REAL
MEXICAN
FOOD

REAL MEXICAN FOOD

Ben Fordham & Felipe Fuentes Cruz
of BENITO'S HAT MEXICAN KITCHEN

photography by Peter Cassidy

LONDON · NEW YORK

ABOUT THE AUTHORS

BEN FORDHAM opened Benito's Hat, a Mexican bar and kitchen, on Goodge Street in 2008; now there are four branches in London. His dream to open a Mexican restaurant began when he lived in Texas and he discovered real Mexican food. From hole-in-the-wall canteens with plastic chairs to fine-dining restaurants, it was all a far cry from what was then being served up in London as Mexican food, but it was particularly the simple, fresh burrito and taco bars that Ben thought London was crying out for. From that point on he began the plan to bring authentic, good-quality, fresh food to his home town at a reasonable price. Ben started moonlighting at a Mexican restaurant while continuing his legal career and shortly afterwards he met Felipe, who had the same dream of bringing great Mexican food to London.

FELIPE FUENTES CRUZ was born in Puebla, Mexico. He and his eight brothers and sisters often had to lend his mother and grandmother a hand when it came to putting food on the table. At 19, he emigrated to the USA where he began his restaurant life. In 2006, he came to London, via a stint in Barcelona, and a year later, Felipe was working in a Mexican restaurant when Ben walked in. They instantly found common ground in their passion for Mexican food. Felipe has been a business partner and head chef of Benito's Hat since it began in 2008. **Visit their website at www.benitos-hat.com**

ABOUT THE PHOTOGRAPHER

PETER CASSIDY is one of Europe's most talented photographers. He specializes in food and travel and his work frequently appears in magazines. For Ryland Peters & Small, he has photographed many books including, most recently, **The Red Hot Chilli Cookbook**.

DEDICATION

We would like to dedicate this book to our families: Siobhan, Ferran and Yasmin, and Kay Lee, Penelope and Beatrice.

SENIOR DESIGNER Megan Smith
COMMISSIONING EDITOR Céline Hughes
HEAD OF PRODUCTION Patricia Harrington
ART DIRECTOR Leslie Harrington
EDITORIAL DIRECTOR Julia Charles

PROP STYLIST Tony Hutchinson
INDEXER Hilary Bird

First published in 2012
by Ryland Peters & Small
20–21 Jockey's Fields,
London WC1R 4BW
and
519 Broadway, 5th Floor,
New York NY 10012

www.rylandpeters.com

UK: 10 9 8 7 6 5 4 3 2 1
US: 10 9 8 7 6 5 4 3 2 1

Text © Ben Fordham and Felipe Fuentes Cruz 2012
Design and photographs © Ryland Peters & Small 2012

UK ISBN: 978-1-84975-258-9
US ISBN: 978-1-84975-342-5

Printed and bound in China

NOTES

• All spoon measurements are level, unless otherwise specified.
• Recipes containing raw or partially cooked egg, or raw fish or shellfish, should not be served to the very young, very old, anyone with a compromised immune system or pregnant women.

contents

Introduction

This book and the Benito's Hat restaurants are born out of mine and Felipe's passion to bring fantastic, simple Mexican food to the British people. From the day we opened our first Hat in July 2008, we have stayed true to our belief in the importance of quality ingredients and cooking everything fresh every day. A visit to Benito's Hat takes your taste buds on a journey from the palm-fringed beaches and turquoise waves of Puerto Vallarta to the bustling heart of Mexico City for a fast, fresh and affordable feast like no other. This book will allow you to make that journey in the comfort of your own home, with a deliberately wide variety of recipes. Some recipes, like the Elote Asado (page 23), are a lesson in simplicity, while others, like the Chiles en Nogada (page 74), require patience and precision, so hopefully you will find something to suit every occasion.

Felipe's education in Mexican food began in his grandmother's kitchen. Since then he has worked in restaurant kitchens in California, Barcelona and now London. He has gained in experience and technique every step of the way and has developed his own style of unique cooking that is a true melting pot of all the influences that he has come across on his wonderful culinary journey.

While my love of cooking and food also began at home, I came to appreciate Mexican food relatively late on. A year spent studying in Austin, Texas showed me the huge gulf between what was available there and what passed for Mexican food in the UK. That year I fell in love with the lady who is now my wife and also with the vibrant, fresh flavours that are at the heart of Mexican cooking.

Benito's Hat sets itself apart from the other Latin American restaurants in the UK with our Puebla-born chef, Felipe, at the helm of the kitchen. Inspired by his native country's famous street food, zingy flavours and rich culinary culture, Felipe has created a menu featuring freshly made burritos, tacos, soups and salads. Authentic recipes for marinades, salsas and beans are given a modern and unique twist by Felipe. On the following pages, Felipe and I give away some of the secrets of the restaurant as well many more recipes that Felipe has developed over 30 years spent in Mexican kitchens.

Tequilas containing barely 50% agave and pre-made lime-juice mixes do not a good margarita make! Here we encourage you to use Tequila made with 100% blue agave and freshly squeezed lime juice as a classic margarita base from which you can create many different delicious cocktails exactly to your taste.

Those of you who already love Mexican food will find new and exciting recipes in the pages of this book. Mexico's food varies from region to region and, as we have already said, Felipe's cooking has taken on influences from many places, so we are sure that even those of you who are very familiar with its cuisine will find things here to surprise and delight you. Those of you who are new to cooking it, please put aside any preconceptions you might have and embrace the beautiful flavours and combinations that this wonderful country and its cuisine have to offer.

Ben Fordham

The Mexican pantry

AVOCADO (SEE ALSO PAGE 103)
Where to start with the wonderful avocado? It contains nearly 20 vitamins and nutrients such as potassium, which helps to relieve high blood pressure. It is also super rich in monounsaturated fats (the good ones).

CORIANDER/CILANTRO (SEE ALSO PAGE 107)
This plant is grown throughout the world and is used both as a herb, through the fresh leaves, and as a spice, by its seeds. The leaves impart a wonderful citrus and even minty flavour to dishes but, beware, it is a herb that divides opinion.

LIMES
The balance of citrus and spice is at the heart of Mexican cooking. Fresh lime juice can be used equally to cut the sweetness in desserts or bring out the individual flavours in a spicy salsa.

TOMATOES
Walk into any vegetable market in Mexico and you will see more varieties of tomato than you can count. Whether you are going for the standard plum or the rippled kidney tomato, give it a good smell before buying and you will know instantly if you are getting something flavourful and fresh.

QUESO FRESCO
This creamy, soft cheese originated in Spain and travelled to Mexico with the earlier settlers. We have used feta as an alternative in several recipes here but if you prefer something milder then Indian paneer is a good bet.

CHILLIES (SEE ALSO PAGE 36)
These are the stars of Mexican cuisine and an essential part of the Mexican diet. The level of heat depends on the concentration of a substance called capsaicin. The most developed species in Mexico is Capsicum Annuum, which includes many varieties ranging in colour, shape, flavour and heat.

JALAPEÑOS (SEE ALSO PAGE 92)
Originally from the Mexican city of Xalapa, Jalapeños can reach up to 7 cm/2¾ inches long and 3 cm/1¼ inches wide at the base. It is a hot chilli but the intensity of the heat can vary widely depending on the terrain and variety of seed.

CHIPOTLE CHILLIES
These are dried, smoked Jalapeños. The name comes from the Nahuatl word "chilpoctli" which means "smoked chilli". They are often found preserved in a sweet adobo sauce or in a paste.

HABANERO CHILLIES
These are serious chillies that really pack a punch. Scotch Bonnets are a different variety of the same species, so they work very well as a substitute.

GUAJILLO CHILLIES
These are not hot but have a delicate fruity flavour. They are dried and made from Mirasol chillies.

TOMATILLOS (SEE ALSO PAGE 104)
Similar to a tomato with a unique tart flavour that is a wonderful addition to many salsas, the fruit is green or purple and surrounded by a papery skin.

CORN
The plant is native to the Americas and was only introduced to Europe in the 17th century. Its origin is said to be the Tehuacán Valley in Mexico which was the heart of the Aztec civilization. It therefore became an integral part of the people's diet.

POMEGRANATE
The look of the bright red seeds of this fruit are reason enough to use them, but they also add a sweetness to citrus salads and some meats.

ALSO ESSENTIAL garlic, onion, fresh ginger, Chiles de Arbol, Serrano chillies, Ancho chillies, sour cream, mango, watermelon, plantain

BEANS

Whether black (turtle) or pinto, beans are a staple of the Mexican diet. They are a great source of protein, fibre and iron. Use them as a side, or beef them up with some fatty cuts of pork and a little heat to make them a meal in their own right.

MASA HARINA

This flour is the product of grinding dried field corn or maize. It forms the base of corn tortillas, as well as being the core ingredient in many sauces.

AVOCADO LEAVES (SEE ALSO PAGE 85)

The avocado tree is known almost everywhere in the world because of its fruit, but the leaves are a wonderful, aromatic addition to many dishes too. The dried leaves give off a smell similar to anise and go well with beans and some stewed meats.

PAPRIKA

This spice is made from grinding together sweet/bell and chilli peppers, so whether it has heat or not depends on the variety you choose. It is used both for its flavour and its deep red colour.

OREGANO

This is a gentle herb that adds a clean, fresh flavour to dishes. For the recipes in this book, we recommend dried Mexican oregano, which has a slightly stronger flavour. It can also be used as a substitute for the harder-to-find epazote.

AGAVE SYRUP (SEE ALSO PAGE 132)

This syrup, or nectar, comes from the sap obtained from the stalk of the agave plant. It is commonly used as a substitute for sugar but its primary purpose in life is for margaritas!

PUMPKIN AND PUMPKIN SEEDS

Using the delicious, buttery flesh of a pumpkin as well as the seeds inside is very satisfying. The two go very well together, as the earthiness of the seeds contrasts beautifully with the delicate flesh. If you are scooping the seeds yourself, wash and dry them thoroughly before using.

MONTEREY JACK CHEESE

This semi-hard cheese has become the standard burrito cheese throughout the world. Its origins are shrouded in debate, but it is likely to have been brought to Monterey, California by Franciscan friars from Spain, via Mexico, in the 1700s.

RICE

Rice is a staple of many Mexican meals. I find that basmati rice is easy to cook and takes on other flavours well.

TEQUILA (SEE ALSO PAGE 135)

This "happy" spirit comes from the region of Jalisco. It is made from the fermented and distilled juice of the agave plant, in particular the blue agave. It is the best known and most representative drink of Mexico in the world. To be called Tequila, the drink must be made in Mexico and contain at least 51% sugars from the agave, but we wouldn't recommend anything except 100% agave.

TORTILLAS

Tortillas are the bread of Mexico. These soft, pillowy delights have been ruined by supermarkets the world over but make yourself a delicate corn tortilla (see page 12) and it will lift any dish.

CINNAMON (SEE ALSO PAGE 114)

Cinnamon has a sweet, woody and spicy flavour. It is native to Sri Lanka but the Mexican version is slightly sweeter.

TAMARIND (SEE ALSO PAGE 129)

Tamarind is a tropical tree, native to eastern Africa but that now exists in much of tropical Asia and Latin America. In Mexico it is grown widely in the states of Michoacán, Guerrero, Oaxaca, Chiapas and even Yucatán, where it is known as "pahch'uuk". It has long been an important part of the traditional diet.

ALSO ESSENTIAL sesame seeds, cloves, evaporated milk, condensed milk, hibiscus flowers (see page 129), Mexican chorizo, epazote (see page 96)

How to make corn tortillas

I grew up watching my grandmother and mother make fresh tortillas every day. They passed on their knowledge and love to me and my family and I hope to do the same with my children. Storebought tortillas are improving all the time, but they can never compete with homemade ones.

300 g/2 cups masa harina
300 ml/1¼ cups warm water
¼ teaspoon sea salt
clean plastic bag
tortilla press (optional; see page 19)

MAKES 10 X 8-CM/3¼-IN. TORTILLAS

1 Put the masa harina, water and salt in a mixing bowl and mix well for 5 minutes. Divide the dough into 10 equal pieces and roll into balls.

2 Place one ball of dough in the middle of the plastic bag and place in the middle of the open tortilla press, if using.

3 Fold the bag in half over the dough. Close the tortilla press and push the handle to compress the dough as much as possible.

4 Open the tortilla press and check that the tortilla is nice and thin. Compress again if necessary. Very carefully peel back the plastic from the top of the dough, making sure the dough does not tear, then loosely replace it. Finally, flip it over and gently peel back the plastic.

If you don't have a tortilla press, pat a large saucepan down on top of the plastic-covered dough repeatedly, pressing down firmly and evenly. Now put aside the pan and pat firmly a few times with the palm of your hand to flatten the dough even further. Gently peel off the plastic as above.

Repeat this process until you have used up all the tortilla dough.

To cook, heat a non-stick frying pan over medium heat, then cook each tortilla for 1 minute. Flip over and cook for another minute until cooked through. To keep the tortillas warm, place them on a clean tea towel and fold the cloth over to cover them.

A good tortilla is not too thick and not too thin. If it is too thin, it will break; if too thick, it won't cook evenly. The best tortilla should fluff up when cooked.

1   2   3

antojitos

SNACKS & STARTERS

totopos
homemade tortilla chips

I know that preparing your own tortilla chips may seem like a bit of a hassle. However, this homemade version puts the storebought variety to shame. Once you've got the hang of the timing, it is really very simple. These chips will lift the flavour of your guacamole or salsa instead of sucking it all away.

vegetable oil, for frying
8 corn tortillas, cut into
   eighths
½ teaspoon sea salt

MAKES LOTS!

Pour some vegetable oil into a deep saucepan until it comes 2 cm/¾ inch up the side of the pan. Set over medium heat and leave until the oil is very hot but not smoking.

Carefully drop in the tortilla triangles, in batches of 10, and fry for about 30 seconds, turning the chips gently and often with tongs to prevent them burning.

Using the tongs or a slotted spoon, remove the chips from the pan and allow to drain on kitchen paper/ paper towels. Repeat the process until all the chips have been fried.

Toss with the salt and serve warm.

pepitas
spiced pumpkin seeds

These irresistible salty snacks provide a great and authentic alternative to the normal nuts and olives. They also make a good ingredient in sauces and dressings, so it's worth getting the hang of making them.

90 g/¾ cup shelled
   pumpkin seeds
¼ teaspoon paprika
a pinch of sea salt
1 teaspoon vegetable oil
1 lime, halved (optional)

MAKES A BOWLFUL

Put the pumpkin seeds in a dry frying pan over low heat. Stir continuously for 10 minutes, taking care not to let them burn.

Remove from the heat, add the paprika, salt and oil and mix well.

Immediately transfer to a bowl to prevent further cooking.

Serve plain or with a squeeze of lime juice. They work well as a snack or as an accompaniment to your meal.

memelitas, rojas y verdes
green & red memelitas

You will find memelitas among all the late-night street vendors throughout cities in Mexico. Try them as a snack, canapé or light lunch.

125 ml/½ cup vegetable oil
½ onion, finely chopped
1 quantity dough from How to Make Corn Tortillas recipe (page 12)
Salsa Verde (page 104)
Salsa Brava (page 100)
200 g/2 cups crumbled feta cheese

clean plastic bag
tortilla press (optional)

MAKES 8

Heat the oil in a small, deep saucepan. Once hot, remove from the heat and add the chopped onion. Set aside until later.

Make the dough using the How to Make Corn Tortillas recipe on page 12 and divide into 8 equal pieces. Roll into balls. Place one ball of dough in the middle of the plastic bag and fold the bag in half over the dough.

Flatten the dough using a tortilla press or, if you don't have a tortilla press, pat a large saucepan down on top of the plastic-covered dough repeatedly, pressing down firmly and evenly. Now put aside the pan and pat firmly a few times with the palm of your hand to flatten the dough even further.

Very carefully peel back the plastic from the top of the dough, making sure the dough does not tear, then loosely replace it. Finally, flip it over and gently peel back the plastic. The disc should be about ½ cm/ ¾ inch thick.

Heat a non-stick frying pan over medium heat, then cook each disc of dough for 1 minute. Flip over and cook for another minute until cooked through, then set aside and allow to cool slightly while you cook the remaining discs.

Take a disc and, using your index finger and thumb, pinch the edge of the tortilla all the way round and make a few pinches in the middle. Repeat with the remaining tortillas.

Return the non-stick frying pan to medium heat. Place a tortilla in the pan, pour 1 teaspoon of the reserved onion oil on top and spread it evenly. Heat for about 1 minute, then spread a little Salsa Verde or Salsa Brava over it. Sprinkle some cheese on top.

Remove from the pan and repeat with all the remaining memelitas. If your pan is big enough you can heat more than one at a time.

Let your guests choose their favourite memelitas.

*

TORTILLA PRESSES are traditional and essential pieces of equipment in Mexican kitchens. If you don't want to invest in one, don't let this stop you from making your own tortillas – a large pan can do the job just as well. Either way, you will need a clean plastic bag to sandwich the dough in before flattening it. A plastic bag works much better than clingfilm/plastic wrap, which tends to stick to itself and the dough.

Every bite of this colourful starter offers crunch as well as a fluffy, cheesy potato filling. It's seriously satisfying. I usually serve it with Guacamole (page 107) or Salsa Verde (page 104).

taquitos dorados de papa con dos quesos
two-cheese fried taquitos

400 g/14 oz. potatoes, peeled and cut into chunks
a pinch of salt
a pinch of dried oregano
100 g/1 cup grated cheddar cheese
16 corn tortillas
vegetable oil, for frying

TO SERVE
1 small head of Romaine lettuce, shredded
200 g/2 cups crumbled feta cheese
Pico de Gallo (page 107)
sour cream

48 cocktail sticks/ toothpicks

MAKES 16

Boil the potatoes until tender but not too soft. Drain and allow to cool in the saucepan.

Add the salt, oregano and cheddar cheese to the potatoes.

Using a fork or potato masher, roughly mash the ingredients together until just combined.

Warm a tortilla in a dry, non-stick frying pan until softened and flexible. When soft, spoon a little of the potato mixture slightly to one side of the middle of the tortilla.

Roll the tortilla into a cylinder and secure it with 3 cocktail sticks/ toothpicks gently pushed through the cylinder. Repeat until all the tortillas have been prepared.

Pour some vegetable oil into a deep frying pan until it comes 2 cm/¾ inch up the side of the pan. Set over medium heat and leave until the oil is very hot but not smoking.

Carefully drop in the taquitos, in batches of 3–4, and fry for about 7–10 minutes, turning them gently and occasionally with tongs to prevent them from burning.

Using the tongs or a slotted spoon, remove the taquitos from the pan and allow to drain on kitchen paper/ paper towels. Repeat the process until all the taquitos have been fried.

Once the taquitos are cool enough to handle, remove the sticks.

TO SERVE
Put a little shredded lettuce on each plate, lay on about 4 taquitos and top with crumbled feta, some Pico de Gallo and sour cream.

Corn snacks are found on street stalls all across Mexico. When I was growing up, corn was the barometer for whether it was going to be a good year or not. If my parents' corn harvest was plentiful, we would begin all our summer meals with one of these dishes.

elote asado
grilled corn on the cob

4 whole corn on the cob, husks and stray strands removed, then thoroughly washed and dried
2 limes, quartered
sea salt
1 teaspoon medium chilli powder/ground red chilli or paprika

SERVES 4

Preheat the grill/broiler to high.

Grill/broil the cobs, turning regularly, for 15–20 minutes or until charred all over.

Remove from the grill/broiler with tongs and rub lime wedges over each cob.

Generously sprinkle each cob with salt and chilli powder/ground chilli or paprika to taste.

esquites oregano sweetcorn

20 g/1½ tablespoons butter
300 g/2 cups sweetcorn kernels
1 fresh Chile de Arbol or Thai green chilli, seeded and cut into long, thin strips
1 teaspoon dried oregano

½ teaspoon sea salt
2 lime wedges
40 g/⅓ cup crumbled feta cheese
2 tablespoons mayonnaise
½ teaspoon paprika

SERVES 2

Melt the butter in a saucepan over high heat, then fry the corn and chilli for 3–4 minutes until they start getting crispy. Add the oregano and salt and cook for 1 minute. Remove from the heat and allow to cool.

Divide the corn between 2 cups and squeeze a lime wedge over each. Top with the crumbled feta and the mayonnaise, then dust the paprika over the top.

camarones a la plancha
grilled shrimp

This is a lovely start to a meal, and making the trip to the fishmonger for the freshest prawns/shrimp is really worth it! The simple accompanying salsa is full of flavour and accentuates, rather than overpowers, the prawns. It's not very dignified but we always suck and crunch the shells between our teeth to get the sauce out. We don't actually eat the shells, but the way the sauce combines with them enhances the flavours.

2 tomatoes
1 tablespoon very finely chopped onion
1 green chilli
1 small bunch of coriander/cilantro, finely chopped
¼ teaspoon sea salt
15 g/1½ tablespoons butter
6 large prawns/shrimp, shell on
5 garlic cloves, very finely chopped

SERVES 2

Put the tomatoes, onion, chilli and 500 ml/2 cups water in a saucepan over high heat. Cover with a lid and bring to the boil, then turn the heat down to low and simmer for about 5–7 minutes.

Drain, then allow to cool for at least 5 minutes before transferring to a food processor with the coriander/cilantro and half the salt. Whizz for 2 minutes and set aside.

Heat a stovetop grill pan or frying pan over medium heat.

Put the butter and prawns/shrimp in the pan and cook for 3–4 minutes or until opaque and cooked through, turning occasionally. Add the garlic and cook for 2 minutes.

Divide the prawns/shrimp between 2 dishes and spoon some of the coriander/cilantro sauce over them. Serve with the remaining sauce on the side for dipping into.

*

LARGE PRAWNS/SHRIMP make such a quick, tasty and versatile snack or light dish. High in protein and low in fat, each little morsel is packed with potential. Grilling/broiling works very well with large or jumbo prawns/shrimp while they are still in their shell, as this allows the meat inside to cook without drying out. It is easy to overcook them, so please use a light touch and watch them carefully for when they turn opaque.

The Gulf of Mexico attracts scores of large prawns/shrimp, so Mexican cooking is full of great recipes to make the best use of this fantastic seafood.

coctel de camarones
Mexican shrimp cocktail

This Mexican twist on the 1980s classic is great fun and suitable for a light snack. Alternatively, dress it up in a cocktail glass and it's ready for your most high-class guests. The fresh juices and cucumber give it a really refreshing flavour and contrast beautifully with the spice of the Worcestershire sauce and Tabasco.

180 g/6 oz. raw, peeled prawns/shrimp
100 g/3½ oz. peeled cucumber
1 small wedge of onion
1 small tomato
1 big tablespoon chopped coriander/cilantro, plus extra to garnish
125 ml/½ cup tomato ketchup
75 ml/⅓ cup lime juice
125 ml/½ cup orange juice
5 drops Worcestershire sauce
5 drops Tabasco sauce
a pinch of sea salt
a pinch of white pepper

TO SERVE
50 g/1¾ oz. avocado flesh, finely chopped
saltine crackers or tortilla chips

SERVES 4

Bring 250 ml/1 cup water to the boil in a saucepan and add the prawns/shrimp.

Cook for 2 minutes or until opaque and cooked through.

Remove from the water with a slotted spoon and reserve the cooking water for later. Set both aside to cool.

Meanwhile, finely chop the cucumber, onion, tomato and coriander/cilantro.

In a bowl, mix the prawns/shrimp, 125 ml/½ cup of the reserved cooking water, the cucumber, onion, tomato, coriander/cilantro, tomato ketchup, lime and orange juice, Worcestershire sauce, Tabasco sauce, salt and pepper. Mix well.

TO SERVE
Divide the mixture between 4 cocktail glasses or small bowls and top with the avocado.

Garnish with a little extra coriander/cilantro and serve with saltine crackers or tortilla chips.

tostadas de frijol
fried tortillas with black beans

These crispy fried tortillas are great as the start to a big feast or as a light meal in their own right. Much of the joy in Mexican food is in friends and family getting together, rolling up their sleeves and tucking in with their hands. That idea really comes out in dishes like this. Strangers don't remain strangers for long when you're eating like this and it's not easy to stay prim and proper!

1 quantity cooked black beans from Frijoles Negros con Hojas de Aguacate (page 88)
250 ml/1 cup vegetable oil
1 onion, cut into large chunks
1 large garlic clove, peeled and bruised
12 corn tortillas

TO SERVE
200 g/2 cups crumbled feta cheese
1 head of Romaine lettuce, shredded
1 avocado, peeled, pitted and cut into strips
Salsa Verde (page 104)

SERVES 4

Put the cooked beans in a food processor and whizz for 3 minutes.

Heat 2 tablespoons of the oil in a frying pan over high heat, then fry the onion and garlic for about 5 minutes or until well browned. The onion and garlic are used only to flavour the oil, so remove them from the oil and discard.

Add the puréed beans to the pan, turn the heat down to low and simmer for 10 minutes. Remove from the heat and set aside to cool until cold.

Pur the remaining oil into a deep frying pan over medium heat. Heat until the oil is very hot but not smoking. Drop in a tortilla and cook for 15 seconds, then turn it over with tongs and cook for 1 minute, using a potato masher (or another metal tool that has a flat end with holes) to hold the tortilla down flat in the oil.

Using the tongs or a slotted spoon, remove the tortilla from the pan and allow to drain on kitchen paper/paper towels. Repeat the process until all the tortillas have been fried.

TO SERVE
Put all fillings in bowls in the middle of the table for everyone to help themselves. Layer up the ingredients over the tortillas: beans, crumbled feta cheese, lettuce, avocado and Salsa Verde.

sopas y ensaladas

SOUPS & SALADS

sopa de calabacitas
chunky vegetable soup

This is one of my mum's recipes and a dish that I remember her preparing over and over again for lunch when I was little. Of all the dishes that she makes, this is one of my favourites and also loved by my wife and children. It is very simple and shows off the fantastic fresh ingredients that were plentiful in all the markets in my home town, and are also readily available outside of Mexico.

TORTILLA STRIPS
8 corn tortillas

SOUP
2 tablespoons olive oil
50 g/⅓ cup finely chopped onion
3 garlic cloves, thinly sliced
500 g/1 generous lb. tomatoes, finely chopped
850 g/2 lbs. courgettes/zucchini, thickly sliced
1 teaspoon sea salt
a pinch of white pepper
1 large bunch of coriander/cilantro, chopped, plus extra to garnish
200 g/2 cups crumbled feta (or grated Monterey Jack or cheddar cheese)

SERVES 4–6

TORTILLA STRIPS
Preheat the oven to 180°C (350°F) Gas 4.

Cut the tortillas into strips about 1 cm/½ inch wide.

Lay the tortilla strips in a single layer on a baking sheet and toast in the preheated oven for 5–7 minutes or until they start to turn golden and crispy. Turn with tongs occasionally to prevent them from sticking together and to ensure that they cook evenly. Set aside.

SOUP
Heat the oil in a saucepan over medium heat, then fry the onion, garlic and tomatoes for 2 minutes.

Add the courgettes/zucchini, salt and pepper and 1 litre/4 cups water and bring to the boil. Turn the heat down and simmer gently for 5 minutes. Remove from the heat and add the coriander/cilantro.

TO SERVE
Divide the soup between 4–6 bowls, top with the tortilla strips and cheese and garnish with coriander/cilantro.

caldo de pollo con verduras
chicken & vegetable soup with mint

This fantastic dish can be used as a light soup or, served with soft, crusty bread, makes a hearty main dish. The aromatic mint adds a wonderful flavour to it. Unlike other versions of chicken soup, we use whole chicken legs or thighs instead of boneless chunks of chicken breast – this renders a richer flavour and texture. If you've never cooked with chayote before, you're in for a nice surprise! See page 44 for more information.

4 whole chicken legs (1–1.5 kg/2¼–3½ lbs.), skin on or off, as preferred
1 chicken stock cube, crushed
1½ teaspoons sea salt
1 chayote (chow chow)
1 large carrot
1 large courgette/zucchini
2 tomatoes
100 g/3½ oz. baby corn (or fresh, canned or frozen corn kernels)
5 sprigs of mint
a pinch of white pepper

SERVES 4

Put the chicken, stock cube, salt and 1.5 litres/6 cups in a large saucepan, bring to the boil and boil for about 10 minutes.

Meanwhile, prepare the vegetables. Peel the chayote and cut into wedges. Peel the carrot and cut it into thick matchsticks. Cut the courgette/zucchini into thick, 5-cm/ 2-inch long matchsticks. Finally, cut the tomatoes into wedges.

Add the prepared chayote, carrot, courgette/zucchini, tomatoes, corn, mint and white pepper to the saucepan and simmer gently for another 10–15 minutes or until the chicken is cooked through.

TO SERVE
Divide the soup between 4 bowls, giving each person an equal amount of chicken.

caldo de pollo
chicken soup

This is a simple, homely dish that is so easy to make. The wonderful broth combines beautifully with the raw, citrusy ingredients. As they are not cooked, they remain firm, fresh and punchy.

about 400 g/14 oz.
   skinless chicken
   breast
1 chicken stock cube,
   crushed
1 teaspoon sea salt
¼ onion
2 green chillies
   (optional)
3 tomatoes
1 medium bunch of
   coriander/cilantro
1 lime, halved

SERVES 4

Put the whole chicken breast, stock cube, salt and 1.5 litres/6 cups water in a large saucepan, bring to the boil and boil for 10 minutes or until the chicken is cooked through.

Meanwhile, prepare the vegetables. Finely chop the onion and chillies, if using, and roughly chop the tomatoes and coriander/cilantro.

Remove the chicken from the broth with a slotted spoon and set aside to cool for 10 minutes, reserving the broth.

Shred the cooked chicken using 2 forks and return it to the saucepan with the broth. Bring to the boil and make sure the chicken is piping hot all the way through.

Take the pan off the heat and stir in the prepared onion, chillies, tomatoes and coriander/cilantro.

TO SERVE
Divide the soup between 4 bowls and squeeze the lime halves over the top before serving.

*

CHILLIES are so integral to Mexican dishes that it's a shame to omit them entirely. If you dislike the heat, experiment with small quantities of different varieties of chilli until you find a heat that suits you.

Removing the seeds from any chilli will reduce its potency, so this is the first thing to do if you're worried. Jalapeños (see page 92) and Serranos are both fresh and quite fiery; dried Ancho and Guajillo are mild; Chipotle can vary from medium to hot so approach with caution; Chile de Arbol can be searing; and Habaneros are for chilli fiends only!

After handling chillies, wash your hands very thoroughly with cold water to prevent any chilli heat getting into your eyes.

lentejas con tocino
lentils with bacon & tomato

This is a wonderfully simple dish that is full of flavour. It can be served as a soup or as a main dish accompanied by some tortillas or slices of your favourite crusty bread.

100 g/1 cup dried green
   lentils
300 g/10 oz. bacon
   slices
4 tomatoes
½ onion
2 garlic cloves
1 tablespoon vegetable
   oil
1 teaspoon sea salt
1 medium bunch of
   coriander/cilantro,
   plus extra to garnish

SERVES 4

Put the lentils and 2 litres/8 cups water in a large saucepan over medium heat. Bring to the boil, then lower the heat and simmer for about 10 minutes.

Meanwhile, prepare the remaining ingredients. Roughly chop the bacon into strips and the tomatoes into chunks. Finely chop the onion, garlic and coriander/cilantro.

In another saucepan, heat the oil and fry the bacon over high heat until dark and crispy.

Turn down the heat to medium, add the onion and garlic and stir for about 20 seconds, then add the tomatoes and cook for 2–3 minutes.

Add the cooked lentils, together with their cooking water and the salt. Bring to the boil, then turn down the heat to low and simmer gently for 10 minutes.

Add the coriander/cilantro and cook for another minute.

Garnish with more coriander/cilantro before serving.

LENTILS are a great source of protein, fibre and iron – they truly are tiny morsels of goodness! I don't believe you should over-complicate them but it is important to season them well. They are rich and satisfying and go with almost anything, and the green ones used in this recipe work especially well with the salty depth of flavour you get from crispy bacon.

Try other colours of lentils too. While green lentils soften but hold their shape well on cooking, red lentils disintegate into a purée and brown lentils stay whole and firm.

ensalada césar

Caesar salad with Parmesan dressing

1 head of Romaine
    lettuce
300 g/10 oz. tomatoes
200 g/6½ oz. feta cheese
8 corn tortillas
100 g/¾ cup shelled
    pumpkin seeds

PARMESAN DRESSING
50 g/⅔ cup grated
    Parmesan cheese
1 garlic clove
200 ml/¾ cup single/
    light cream
80 ml/⅓ cup olive oil
80 ml/⅓ cup vegetable
    oil
80 ml/⅓ cup mayonnaise
1 large bunch of
    coriander/cilantro,
    chopped
a pinch of sea salt
a pinch of white pepper

SERVES 4

This is a Mexican twist on the Italian–American classic, said to have originated at the hands of an Italian chef in California in the 1920s. It is only a short trip down the road from there to the Mexican border-town of Tijuana where there are strong Italian communities and legend has it this is where the Mexican version was first made.

Preheat the oven to 180°C (350°F) Gas 4.

Prepare the ingredients for the salad. Thickly slice the lettuce leaves. Cut the tomatoes into wedges. Crumble the feta into small pieces. Cut the tortillas into strips about 1 cm/½ inch wide.

Lay the tortilla strips in a single layer on a baking sheet and toast in the preheated oven for 5–7 minutes or until they start to turn golden and crispy. Turn with tongs occasionally to prevent them from sticking together and to ensure that they cook evenly. Set aside.

Put the pumpkin seeds in a dry frying pan over low heat. Stir continuously for 10 minutes, taking care not to let them burn. Remove from the heat and set aside.

PARMESAN DRESSING
Put 200 ml/¾ cup water and the remaining dressing ingredients in a food processor and whizz until smooth and creamy – 2–3 minutes. If it is too thick, add a little more water.

TO SERVE
Divide the lettuce and tomatoes between 4 bowls, drizzle the dressing over them and top with the tortilla strips, feta and toasted pumpkin seeds.

ensalada de jícama
jicama & cucumber salad

As a young boy I used to pick jicama, or yam bean roots, in the fields behind our house. They grow wild in many regions of Mexico where they are eaten raw as a snack. Here in London, another Mexican chef and I played with the idea of using jicama in a salad. Its fresh taste pairs well with peanuts and earthy Manchego cheese.

50 g/⅓ cup shelled, skinned peanuts
1 jicama (yam bean root)
1 cucumber
1 medium bunch of coriander/cilantro
1 tomato (optional)
1 lime, halved
2 lemons, halved
a pinch of paprika
30 g/⅓ cup grated Manchego or Parmesan cheese

SERVES 2

Put the peanuts in a dry non-stick frying pan over medium heat. Toast, stirring continuously, for 7–10 minutes or until browned. Remove from the heat and set aside.

Prepare the vegetables. Peel the jicama and cucumber, then chop into thick matchsticks. Finely chop the coriander/cilantro and tomato.

Put the jicama, cucumber, coriander/cilantro, tomato and peanuts in a big bowl. Squeeze the lime and lemons over the top and add the paprika. Mix well. Sprinkle the cheese over everything just before serving.

ensalada de chayote
chayote & grapefruit salad

Chayote (or chow chow as it is sometimes known) is a member of the gourd family. It has a mild taste but this means that it happily absorbs and takes on the flavours of the lime, paprika and salt in this salad. The goal here is to cook it just enough to soften it but still leave it with a delightful crunch.

3 tablespoons shelled pumpkin seeds
1 chayote (chow chow)
1 pink grapefruit or orange
1 small bunch of coriander/cilantro, chopped
1 tablespoon lime juice
2 tablespoons olive oil
¼ red onion, very thinly sliced
20 g/3 cups rocket/ arugula
a pinch of paprika
a pinch of sea salt

SERVES 2

Put the pumpkin seeds in a dry frying pan over low heat. Stir continuously for 7–10 minutes, taking care not to let them burn. Remove from the heat and set aside.

Put the whole chayote in a saucepan, and cover with water. Bring to the boil, then simmer for 10 minutes. Drain and set aside to cool slightly.

When the chayote has cooled, cut it in half, remove the stone and cut each half into thin wedges.

Peel the grapefruit, remove the bitter white pith and cut the flesh into neat segments.

TO SERVE
Mix all the ingredients together in a large bowl.

*

CHAYOTE is a pale green, furrowed fruit, also known as a chow chow, christophene, mirliton or vegetable pear. In fact it is similar in shape to and slightly larger than a big pear, but its subtle flavour is closer to that of cucumber. It has featured in Mexican cuisine since the time of the Aztecs and Mayans and is now also popular in the USA and UK.

Chayote can be eaten raw or cooked, when it should be prepared as you would a summer squash.

ensalada de habas
spicy broad/fava bean salad

During my career I have worked with chefs from all over Mexico but it was a chef in London who first introduced me to this wonderful salad. The spicy, pickled Jalapeños provide a fantastic contrast to the beautiful fresh broad/fava beans. It surprises and delights me that, having spent many decades cooking Mexican food around the world, I am still discovering new dishes from my home country.

400 g/14 oz. fresh
    broad/fava beans
¼ red onion
3 tomatoes
1 medium bunch of
    coriander/cilantro
25–50 g/2–4 tablespoons
    pickled chopped
    Jalapeños (depending
    on how spicy you
    like it)
1 tablespoon of the
    vinegar from the
    Jalapeños
freshly squeezed juice
    of 1 lime
2 tablespoons olive oil
¼ teaspoon sea salt
¼ teaspoon dried
    oregano

SERVES 4

Remove the broad/fava beans from their pods but leave them in their individual skins.

Steam the beans for 3–4 minutes until just tender. Run them under cold water to cool them down, then peel off the pale skin from all of them and discard.

Prepare the remaining ingredients. Finely chop the onion, roughly chop the tomatoes and tear off the leaves of the coriander/cilantro.

Put the beans, chopped onion, tomatoes, coriander/cilantro and Jalapeños in a large salad bowl and add the Jalapeño vinegar, lime juice, olive oil, salt and oregano.

Mix well and serve.

platillos fuertes

MAIN DISHES

chilaquiles rojos
fried corn tortillas
with chilli tomato sauce & cheese

This is a very traditional Mexican dish but one which has its variations and twists in every region of Mexico. Chilaquiles are usually served for breakfast or lunch and are a great way to make use of any leftover tortillas and salsas, of which there are always plenty in a Mexican kitchen!

vegetable oil, for frying
10 corn tortillas, cut into eighths
2 tomatoes
5 dried Chiles de Arbol (or other hot dried red chillies), seeded and stalks removed
1 teaspoon paprika
½ onion, finely chopped
2 medium eggs
a pinch of sea salt
100 g/1 cup grated cheddar cheese

SERVING SUGGESTION
refried black or pinto beans (see pages 88–91)

SERVES 4

Pour some vegetable oil into a deep saucepan until it comes 2 cm/¾ inch up the side of the pan. Set over medium heat and leave until the oil is very hot but not smoking.

Carefully drop in the tortilla triangles, in batches of 10, and fry for about 30 seconds, turning the chips gently and often with tongs to prevent them from burning.

Using the tongs or a slotted spoon, remove the chips from the pan and allow to drain on kitchen paper/paper towels. Repeat the process until all the chips have been fried. Reserve the oil.

Place 500 ml/2 cups water, the tomatoes and chillies in a saucepan and boil for 5 minutes.

Allow to cool for 10 minutes, then transfer all of it to a food processor with the paprika and whizz for 2 minutes or until smooth. Set aside.

Take 1 tablespoon of the reserved cooking oil and put in a large saucepan over medium heat.

Add the tortilla chips and onions to the pan, then add the eggs. Using a large spoon, very gently stir the mixture for 1 minute until the egg is cooked, but be careful not to break the fried tortilla chips.

Add the blended sauce, as well as the salt and cook for 3–5 minutes or until the sauce is heated through – do not overcook it otherwise the tortillas will turn soggy. They need to be mixed well with the sauce but still retain a little of their crunchiness.

Preheat the grill/broiler to medium.

Transfer the chilaquiles to an ovenproof dish and sprinkle the cheese over the top. Grill/broil for 1–2 minutes to melt the cheese.

SERVING SUGGESTION
Serve with refried beans, if you like.

huevos con chorizo
scrambled eggs with chorizo

Just as they are here in London, eggs are a very popular way to start the day in Mexico. They are usually scrambled ("huevos revueltos") and mixed with a variety of ingredients. Here we are using chorizo and the key is to make sure that you don't scrimp on its quality. Mexican chorizo usually comes as ground meat but for this recipe we use the Spanish sausage found in most supermarkets and it works very well. Most chorizo is a deep reddish colour and the colour seeps out in to the eggs to give them a lovely orange tint. There is also a fantastic green chorizo in Mexico which is made with a combination of tomatillos, chillies and garlic – it is worth trying it if you ever get the chance.

4 medium eggs
1 teaspoon olive oil
100 g/3½ oz. chorizo,
  finely sliced
¼ onion, finely chopped
50 g/½ cup grated
  Monterey Jack or
  cheddar cheese

SERVING SUGGESTION
flour tortillas
refried black or pinto
  beans (see pages
  88–91)
Salsa Brava (page 100)
  or other salsa of your
  choice

SERVES 2

Break the eggs into a bowl and beat well with a fork.

Put the oil in a non-stick frying pan over medium heat – you only need a very small amount because the chorizo will release some of its own oils on cooking.

Add the chorizo and fry for about 20 seconds, then add the onions and fry for another 20 seconds, stirring continuously.

Add the eggs and scramble, stirring to break up the eggs, for 1–2 minutes.

Remove from the heat and sprinkle the cheese over the top.

SERVING SUGGESTION
Serve with warm tortillas, refried beans and your favourite salsa, if you like. Personally, I like a bit of a kick in the morning so I go with Salsa Brava every time.

How to make a burrito

Burritos are the core of what we do at Benito's Hat. We serve bespoke, gourmet burritos to thousands of very satisfied people in the UK every week so we feel pretty sure that we know what we are doing here!

"Burrito" literally means "little donkey" and was traditionally a way to use up everything in the larder by packing it into a tortilla. It has taken on many influences, especially from Texas and California, and here I'm showing you a recipe that is a true hybrid of my culinary education, from Mexico, to California, to Spain and, finally, to the UK, which I now call home.

I have chosen one of our favourite combinations of black beans (page 88), Birria de Res (page 57), Guacamole (page 107), Pico de Gallo (page 107), grated cheese, shredded lettuce, sour cream and rice for the signature Benito's Hat burrito. However, there are hundreds of combinations of burrito that you can make using the recipes in this book. By combining different meat fillings (such as the chicken from the recipe on page 66) with different salsas, you will have a new meal every time.

When you have chosen and prepared your fillings, you are ready to put your burrito together!

Prepare the tortilla

Place a dry frying pan over high heat. Warm a tortilla for about 20–30 seconds on each side or until softened. Transfer to a board or plate. Now layer up the ingredients, one by one, roughly across the middle of the tortilla. You're ready to assemble your first burrito!

Assemble the burrito

1 Put one hand on each side of the tortilla and lift up the sides.

2 Fold the sides over the filling to nearly conceal it.

3 Holding the sides down over the filling, use your thumbs to bring the front of the tortilla up over the filling too.

4 Gently tuck this front flap under the filling, rolling the burrito gently to coax it and the filling into a cylinder shape. Roll up the burrito with the palm of your hand. Now enjoy!

birria de res

slow-cooked beef with ginger

1 kg/2¼ lbs. diced beef
2 bay leaves
1 tablespoon vegetable
   oil
2 tablespoons finely
   chopped coriander/
   cilantro
2 tablespoons finely
   chopped onions
1 tablespoon lime juice
sea salt and ground
   black pepper

SAUCE
1 Guajillo chilli, seeded
   and stalks removed
2 tomatoes, chopped
1 garlic clove, peeled
¼ onion, finely chopped
1 tablespoon dried
   oregano
2 cm/1 inch fresh
   ginger, peeled
1 teaspoon ground
   cumin
2 tablespoons paprika
1 garlic clove
½ teaspoon ground
   cinnamon
1 teaspoon white
   vinegar

SERVES 6

This dish is a bit time-consuming, but for all you beef-lovers it is more than worth all the preparation time. It is full of flavour and, once made, can be used to produce two different dishes. As described below, it is designed as a burrito filling, but by adding extra water to the sauce, you can turn it into a great stew. Be sure to add the onion, coriander/cilantro and a squeeze of lime at the end to unlock the flavour of the birria. It'll transport you straight to the mercados in the state of Jalisco where this dish originates.

Put the beef, bay leaves, 1 teaspoon salt and 2 litres/8 cups water in a large saucepan over high heat. Bring to the boil, then turn the heat down to low and gently simmer for about 2–2½ hours until the meat falls apart easily when pulled.

Drain the cooked beef in a colander and reserve the cooking liquid. Set both aside while you make the sauce.

SAUCE
Put the chilli, tomatoes, garlic, onion and 500 ml/2 cups water in a saucepan over high heat and cover with water. Bring to the boil, then turn the heat down to medium and simmer for 5 minutes.

Remove from the heat and transfer to a food processor with all the remaining sauce ingredients and 1 teaspoon salt. Whizz until smooth – 2–4 minutes. Season with pepper.

TO FINISH
Heat the oil in a large frying pan. Add the sauce and sauté for 5 minutes. Add the beef and 250 ml/1 cup of the reserved cooking liquid and bring to the boil. Half-cover with a lid, turn the heat down to low and cook for 10–15 minutes or until the sauce has thickened.

TO SERVE
Mix together the coriander/cilantro, onion and lime juice and sprinkle over the meat.

Assemble the burrito according to the instructions on page 54.

taco de camarón
shrimp tacos
with butter, garlic & paprika

15 g/1 tablespoon butter
2 garlic cloves, chopped
200 g/6½ oz. shelled raw or cooked prawns/shrimp
a pinch of paprika
4 x 15-cm/6-in. corn or flour tortillas

TO SERVE
150 g/2 cups shredded Romaine lettuce
Pico de Gallo (page 107)
Chipotle Garlic Mayonnaise (page 61)
1 lemon, cut into wedges

SERVES 2

Melt the butter in a frying pan over low heat and fry the garlic, prawns/shrimp and paprika for 2–4 minutes, stirring occasionally, until the prawns/shrimp are cooked through.

Place a dry frying pan over high heat. Warm each tortilla for about 20–30 seconds on each side.

TO SERVE
Layer up the ingredients over the tortillas: lettuce, Pico de Gallo, prawns/shrimp and Chipotle Garlic Mayonnaise. Serve with lemon wedges to squeeze over.

Prawns/shrimp are one of my favourite seafood. Even though my home town of Puebla is inland, fresh fish is delivered daily to the market and seafood restaurants are everywhere. This dish takes me right back to happy times with my brothers, sitting out in the sunshine with tacos and a cold beer.

taco de pescado
fish tacos

Fish tacos are associated with Baja California, the Mexican peninsula with an incredible coastline that stretches for miles. Fishing is the main source of livelihood there and you can watch fresh seafood being brought in almost all day. For this recipe we recommend tilapia: it is sustainable and its firm, white flesh stands up well to being battered and fried.

CHIPOTLE GARLIC MAYONNAISE
2 garlic cloves, peeled
250 ml/1 cup
mayonnaise
3–6 tablespoons
Chipotle chilli paste

FISH
125 g/1 cup plain/
all-purpose flour
2 teaspoons paprika
2 teaspoons dried
oregano
1 teaspoon dried
marjoram
2 teaspoons ground
cumin
½ teaspoon sea salt
½ teaspoon ground
white pepper
4 tilapia fish fillets
vegetable oil, for frying
8 x 15-cm/6-in. corn or
flour tortillas

TO SERVE
a handful of shredded
Romaine lettuce
Pico de Gallo (page 107)
1 lemon, cut into
wedges

SERVES 4

CHIPOTLE GARLIC MAYONNAISE
Put all the ingredients in a food processor and whizz for 3 minutes. Set aside.

FISH
Put the flour, paprika, oregano, marjoram, cumin, salt, pepper and 250 ml/1 cup water in a large bowl and whisk together until very smooth and slightly thicker than double/ heavy cream.

Cut each tilapia fillet into 2 pieces.

Gently lower each portion of fish into the batter and make sure it is well coated. Set aside on a plate.

Pour some vegetable oil into a large, deep frying pan until it comes 2 cm/ ¾ inch up the side of the pan. Set over medium heat and leave until the oil is very hot but not smoking.

Using a slotted spoon, lower the portions of fish gently into the oil. Cook for 1–2 minutes on each side, depending on the thickness. Work in small batches – the fish should have plenty of room in the oil to fry evenly.

Using the tongs or a slotted spoon, remove the fish from the pan and allow to drain on kitchen paper/ paper towels. Repeat the process until all the portions have been fried.

Place a dry frying pan over high heat. Warm each tortilla for about 20–30 seconds on each side.

TO SERVE
Layer up the ingredients over the tortillas: lettuce, Pico de Gallo, the chipotle garlic mayonnaise and a portion of fish. Serve with the lemon wedges to squeeze over.

tacos de pollo
chipotle chicken tacos

Although tacos are at the heart of Mexican cooking, chicken is not as common a filling as pork or beef. Ben and I developed this recipe for Benito's Hat and it has proved to be by far the most popular dish that we do.

400 g/14 oz. chicken breast fillets

8 x 15-cm/6-in. corn or flour tortillas

CHIPOTLE MARINADE

1 tablespoon Chipotle chilli paste

1 teaspoon ground cinnamon

1 teaspoon ground cumin

3 garlic cloves

1 tablespoon dried oregano

1 tablespoon paprika

½ teaspoon sea salt

125 ml/½ cup vegetable oil

TO SERVE

a handful of shredded Romaine lettuce

Pico de Gallo (page 107)

sour cream

SERVES 4

CHIPOTLE MARINADE

Put all the ingredients and 125 ml/ ½ cup water in a food processor and whizz until smooth. Put the chicken breast in a bowl, add the marinade and mix well. Cover, refrigerate and marinate for 2–4 hours.

When you are ready to start cooking, preheat the grill/broiler to high.

Grill/broil the chicken for about 10 minutes, turning halfway through, until cooked through. Cut it into strips.

Place a dry frying pan over high heat. Warm each tortilla for about 20–30 seconds on each side.

TO SERVE

Layer up the ingredients over the tortillas: lettuce, Pico de Gallo, sour cream and the chicken.

tacos de tofu
tofu tacos

Tofu is not something that is eaten much in Mexico. However, not least because my wife is a vegetarian, it is something that I have come to cook with a great deal since coming to London. It is very healthy and its unique texture adds another dimension to many dishes. It also combines very well with a bit of heat. Pico de Gallo is the perfect accompaniment to these tacos, but you could serve them with sour cream too, if you like.

400 g/14 oz. tofu
½ red onion
1 red sweet/bell pepper
1 yellow sweet/bell pepper
2 garlic cloves
1 fresh Jalapeño (or a couple of Thai green chillies for more heat)
20 g/1½ tablespoons butter
½ teaspoon dried oregano
¼ teaspoon sea salt
¼ teaspoon ground white pepper
8 x 15-cm/6-in. corn or flour tortillas

TO SERVE
Pico de Gallo (page 107)

SERVES 4

First, prepare the ingredients. Cut the tofu into strips about 5 cm/2 inches long. Cut the onion and sweet/bell peppers into strips and thinly slice the garlic and Jalapeño.

Melt the butter in a frying pan over high heat, then fry the tofu for about 5 minutes.

Add the onion, sweet/bell peppers, garlic, oregano, salt and pepper and fry for 5 minutes.

The tofu should be brown and a little crispy at the edges and the peppers should still have a little crunch.

Stir in the chopped Jalapeño.

Place a dry frying pan over high heat. Warm each tortilla for about 20–30 seconds on each side.

TO SERVE
Spoon the ingredients over the tortillas and serve with Pico de Gallo.

*

TOFU, or bean curd, is made from soya beans and is most commonly used in Asian cuisine. It's not only a healthy alternative to meat – it's a good source of protein, cholesterol-free and high in calcium – but it's also quite bland and therefore perfect for taking on any stronger flavours that it's cooked with.

As marinades work especially well with tofu, try making the tacos on page 62 using tofu instead of chicken and see how flavourful it becomes from the chipotle marinade.

quesadilla de pollo
chicken quesadillas

The word "quesadilla" comes from "queso" (cheese) and "tortilla", as these basic ingredients are at the core of this dish. The tortilla must be cooked until crisp but not burnt, and the cheese inside must be melted. Just like burritos and tacos, quesadillas can be the base for an infinite number of fillings so that you can experiment with combinations of fillings. Kids love the way the melted cheese glues everything together inside.

Chipotle Marinade (page 62)
400 g/14 oz. chicken breast fillets
4 x 26-cm/10-in. flour tortillas
200 g/2 cups grated Monterey Jack or cheddar cheese

SERVING SUGGESTION
Guacamole (page 107)
sour cream
Pico de Gallo (page 107)

SERVES 4

Make the Chipotle Marinade as described on page 62.

If the chicken fillets are very thick, flatten them slightly with a rolling pin. Put in a bowl, add the marinade and mix well. Cover, refrigerate and marinate for 2–4 hours.

When you are ready to start cooking, preheat the grill/broiler to high.

Grill/broil the chicken for 10 minutes, turning halfway through, until cooked through.

Lay the tortillas in front of you on a clean work surface. Divide the cheese and chicken between the tortillas, arranging them in a wide strip down the middle. Fold a third of the tortilla over the filling, then fold the opposite third over that.

Place a dry stovetop grill pan or frying pan over high heat. Put one quesadilla in the hot pan, allow to brown for about 1 minute, then gently flip it over and toast the other side. Repeat with the remaining quesadillas.

SERVING SUGGESTION
Cut each quesadilla diagonally into 4. Serve with Guacamole, sour cream and Pico de Gallo, if you like.

pierna de puerco adobada
adobo roasted pork

1.5-kg/3¼ lbs. boneless pork leg or shoulder, rolled and tied
1 baguette
sea salt and ground white pepper

ADOBO MARINADE
50 g/1½ Guajillo chillies, seeded and stalks removed
2 teaspoons ground cumin
2 teaspoons ground cinnamon
1½ tablespoons hot chilli powder or paprika
3 tablespoons honey
50 ml/3 tablespoons white wine vinegar
2 garlic cloves, peeled
¼ onion, peeled

SPAGHETTI BLANCO
250 g/9 oz. spaghetti
50 g/3 tablespoons butter
¼ onion, finely chopped
2 garlic cloves, finely chopped
1 large bunch of parsley, finely chopped
500 ml/2 cups single/light cream

SERVES 4–6

I come from the state of Puebla in Mexico where it gets quite cold in the evenings. When it's cold like this, families eat dishes designed to warm the body as well as the soul. This pork dish does exactly that and is often cooked during the festive season. It's also very popular to cook it, allow it to cool, then use it as a filling for a "torta" (a type of Mexican sandwich).

Put the pork on a chopping board, fatty side up. Using a sharp knife, score diagonal lines about 1 cm/½ inch deep across the fat. Swivel the pork around 90° and score diagonal lines in the fat in the opposite direction to create a chequered pattern.

ADOBO MARINADE
Put all the ingredients, 1 generous teaspoon salt, a pinch of pepper and 500 ml/2 cups water in a food processor and whizz for 2–3 minutes or until the mixture is creamy. Put the pork in a large bowl, add the adobo marinade and roll the meat in it until it is well coated. Cover and put in the fridge for 3 hours.

15 minutes before you are ready to start cooking, preheat the oven to 150°C (300°F) Gas 2.

Put the pork in a roasting dish and pour the remaining adobo marinade over it. Cover with foil and roast in the preheated oven for 2 hours.

After 2 hours, remove the foil, return to the oven uncovered and roast for a further 30 minutes.

SPAGHETTI BLANCO
Shortly before the pork has finished cooking, cook the pasta according to the manufacturer's instructions but remove from the heat 2 minutes before time and drain.

Melt the butter in a large saucepan over high heat, then fry the onion, garlic and parsley for 1 minute.

Add the pasta to the pan and heat for 3 minutes, stirring occasionally. Remove from the heat and stir in the cream and ¼ teaspoon pepper.

Carve the pork into thick slices and serve with the pasta and a slice of baguette. Pour some of the juice from the roasting dish over the meat.

barbacoa de cordero
slow-cooked lamb

This lamb barbacoa was my dad's favourite dish. Since arriving in London I have cooked it many times for family, friends and for the restaurant and everyone has always loved it. Many people have been introduced to the depth of flavours of real interior Mexican food with this recipe, as the slow cooking allows each individual ingredient to really penetrate the meat. We offer it as a seasonal dish every year at Benito's Hat and it has proved extremely popular.

1½ tablespoons ground avocado leaves
2 teaspoons sea salt
1-kg/2¼-lb. shoulder of lamb, bone in
¼ onion, finely chopped
1 medium bunch of coriander/cilantro, finely chopped

SERVING SUGGESTION
6 corn tortillas
1 lime, quartered
basmati rice
Salsa de Aguacate (page 103) or Salsa Verde (page 104)
Frijoles Refritos con Paprika (page 91)

SERVES 2–3

Preheat the oven to 180°C (350°F) Gas 4.

Mix the avocado leaves, salt and 80 ml/¼ cup water in a small bowl.

Put the lamb on a rack inside a medium roasting tray and rub the avocado leaf mixture all over it. Pour any excess mixture over the top.

Pour 125 ml/½ cup water into the bottom of the roasting tray.

Cover the lamb with aluminium foil and seal tightly around the edges of the roasting tray, making sure there are no gaps. Roast in the preheated oven for 2½ hours.

Mix the onion and coriander/cilantro together in a small bowl and serve with the roasted lamb.

SERVING SUGGESTION
Place a dry frying pan over high heat. Warm each tortilla for about 20–30 seconds on each side.

Put the lamb in the middle of the table together with the lime wedges, the rice, beans, warm tortillas, Salsa de Aguacate and Frijoles Refritos con Paprika. Get stuck in!

carnitas
pork "little meats"

In Spanish, "carnitas" means little meats and this traditional Mexican dish is made with pork. You can use almost any cut of pork to make this at home. I have chosen pork ribs and pork shoulder steak because I love their contrasting textures and the ribs are great to chew off the bones. The shoulder steak is a pure, lean meat and a good foil for the ribs. We have our own version of carnitas at Benito's Hat but that recipe remains a very closely guarded secret that Ben and I will take to our graves. The version given here features a couple of ingredients that may come as a surprise!

500 g/1 lb. 2 oz. pork ribs/spareribs
500 g/1 lb. 2 oz. pork shoulder steaks
250 g/9 oz. pork lard
2 oranges
250 ml/1 cup cola drink
250 ml/1 cup whole milk
1¼ teaspoons coarse sea salt

SERVING SUGGESTION
flour tortillas
refried black or pinto beans (see pages 88–91)
basmati rice
Salsa Borracha (page 104) or Salsa Diabla (page 103)

SERVES 4

Put the pork, lard and 1.5 litres/6 cups water in a large saucepan or casserole dish over medium heat. Partially cover with a lid and cook for 1 hour.

Meanwhile, grate the zest from 1 orange, then cut it in half and cut each half into 4 segments.

After 1 hour, add the orange zest and segments, cola, milk and 1 teaspoon of the salt to the saucepan. Turn the heat down to low and cook for about 30–40 minutes. A froth will form on the surface but it will subside.

When it is ready, the pork will easily pull away from the bone. Drain the meat and discard the orange segments. Allow the meat to cool for 30 minutes.

Meanwhile, preheat the oven to 180°C (350°F) Gas 4.

Grate the zest from the second orange and mix well with the remaining salt.

Lay out the pork on a rack in a roasting dish. If you don't have a rack, scatter the pork directly in a roasting dish (and you will have to turn the meat halfway through cooking). Scatter the orange-salt mixture evenly over the pork.

Roast in the preheated oven for 25–30 minutes. The meat should be brown and crispy on the outside.

SERVING SUGGESTION
Serve with warm tortillas, refried beans, rice and Salsa Borracha or Salsa Diabla if you can handle it!

chiles en nogada
stuffed poblano chillies

4 Poblano chillies (or sweet/bell peppers)
200 g/7 oz. minced/ground pork
1/3 onion, finely chopped
2 garlic cloves, crushed
2 pears, peeled, cored and finely chopped
1/2 apple, peeled, cored and finely chopped
1 plantain (or banana), peeled and finely chopped
100 g/2/3 cup dried apricots
50 g/1/3 cup chopped walnuts
100 g/2/3 cup chopped almonds
100 g/2/3 cup raisins
1/4 teaspoon ground cinnamon
vegetable oil, for frying
6 eggs, separated
flour, to sprinkle
sea salt and ground white pepper
pomegranate seeds, to serve
chopped coriander/cilantro, to serve

WALNUT SAUCE
50 g/2/3 cup grated cheddar cheese
100 ml/1/2 cup single/light cream
100 ml/1/3 cup milk
50 g/1/3 cup chopped walnuts

SERVES 4

This festive dish originated in my native state of Puebla and is linked to the Independence of Mexico. It is said to have been prepared for the first time to entertain Agustín de Iturbide who was Emperor of the new nation of Mexico. The name comes from the Spanish word for the walnut tree, "nogal".

Remove the stalks from the chillies. If you have a gas hob, hold each chilli with metal tongs and place directly over the gas flame. Rotate for 10 minutes or until evenly blackened. Transfer to a bowl and cover with cold water. If you don't have a gas hob, roast the chillies in an oven preheated to 200°C (400°F) Gas 6 for 15 minutes, turning occasionally.

Keeping the chillies under water, rub the skin until it all flakes off. Make a small hole in the flesh with your finger and open it up slightly. Wash out the seeds and white membrane.

Heat 50 ml/1/4 cup vegetable oil in a frying pan over medium heat and fry the pork for 5 minutes or until well done. Add the onion and garlic and fry for 1 minute. Add the pears, apple, plantain, apricots, nuts, raisins, cinnamon, salt and pepper and fry for 7–10 minutes or until the cinnamon smells fragrant and the mixture starts to stick to the pan. Add 125 ml/1/2 cup water and cook for 1–2 minutes or until evaporated.

Divide the stuffing between each chilli by pushing it through the hole, then press the hole closed and sprinkle flour all over the chillies.

Whisk the egg whites with an electric whisk until soft peaks form. Add the yolks and a pinch of salt and whisk briefly to combine.

Pour some vegetable oil into a small frying pan until it comes 2 cm/3/4 inch up the side of the pan. Set over medium heat and leave until the oil is very hot but not smoking.

Dip a chilli in the batter until evenly coated. Carefully transfer to the hot oil and fry for 1–2 minutes, spooning hot oil over it continuously. Rotate it with tongs and fry for another 1–2 minutes. Using the tongs or a slotted spoon, remove the chillies from the pan and pat dry with kitchen paper/paper towels. Repeat the process until all the chillies have been fried.

WALNUT SAUCE
Put the cheese, cream, milk and walnuts in a food processor and whizz for 3 minutes.

Serve each chilli with the walnut sauce and sprinkle pomegranate seeds and coriander/cilantro on top.

tamales de puerco
pork tamales

500 g/1 lb. 2 oz. boneless pork leg or shoulder, cut into large chunks
2 bay leaves
sea salt and ground white pepper

GUAJILLO SAUCE
¼ onion, chopped
2 garlic cloves, peeled
300 g/10 oz. tomatoes
3 Guajillo chillies, seeded and stalks removed
1½ tablespoons paprika
1 teaspoon ground cumin
½ tablespoon dried oregano
2 tablespoons masa harina
125 ml/½ cup warm water
2 tablespoons vegetable oil

MASA
300 g/3 cups masa harina
1 tablespoon baking powder

TO ASSEMBLE
10 corn husks, soaked in 1 litre/4 cups warm water for 10 minutes, then drained
300 g/3 cups grated Monterey Jack or cheddar cheese

MAKES 10

Tamales are little bundles of stuffed corn dough traditionally served at Christmas and New Year. The parcel is wrapped in a corn husk or banana leaf (depending on the region) and is said to symbolize the baby Jesus. My mum always makes pork tamales during the festive season and I have based my recipe on hers.

Put the pork, bay leaves, 1 teaspoon salt and 1.5 litres/6 cups water in a large saucepan, bring to the boil and simmer over low heat for 1½ hours. Drain (reserving the cooking liquid for later), transfer to a bowl and allow to cool.

GUAJILLO SAUCE
Put the onion, garlic, tomatoes, chillies and 750 ml/3 cups water in a pan, bring to the boil and simmer over low heat for 5 minutes. Transfer to a food processor with 1 tablespoon salt, the paprika, cumin, oregano and a pinch of pepper and whizz for 2 minutes. Mix the masa harina into the warm water until combined. Heat the oil in a frying pan, pour in the sauce, bring to the boil and cook for 5 minutes. Turn the heat down to low, add the masa-water mixture, stir and cook for 5 minutes.

MASA
Put the masa harina and 1 teaspoon salt in a bowl and mix. Add 500 ml/ 2 cups of the reserved cooking liquid and knead for 5 minutes. Add the baking powder and knead for 1 minute. Divide into 10 equal portions.

TO ASSEMBLE
Shred the cooled pork in its bowl, add 1½ cups of the sauce and mix.

Lay out a soaked corn husk (if it is not flat, tear the outside edges a little so that it will stay flat). Put a portion of masa on the husk and flatten with your hand until ½ cm/ ¼ inch thick and an oval shape. Put a line of the pork mixture (about 50 g/ 1¾ oz.) along the middle of the masa. Take one side of the husk and roll over the masa, tucking it in on the other side. You should now have a cylinder. Take the excess husk at one end, fold it under the tamale and tuck in. Leave the other end open.

Put the tamales in a steamer, sealed end down. They should not be too closely packed. Cover tightly with foil, cover with a lid and steam for 1½ hours over medium heat. Check every 30 minutes and add water if needed.

Remove from the heat, open each parcel but leave in the husk. Cover with the remaining sauce, scatter the cheese over the top and grill/ broil until the cheese has melted.

calabaza con acelgas
roasted pumpkin with chard & mushrooms

This is a great autumnal dish that illustrates the development of modern Mexican cooking. It combines ingredients that have been used as staples for hundreds of years, and puts them together in an exciting new way. This recipe is a product of much time sitting in kitchens and homes of Mexican chefs working all over the world. We love to talk and share our experiences about the new flavour combinations we have discovered.

½ medium pumpkin of 1–1.5 kg/2–3 lbs.
4 tablespoons olive oil
a pinch of dried oregano
½ teaspoon ground cumin
2 dried Guajillo chillies, seeded and stalks removed
200 g/6½ oz. Swiss chard (or spinach)
200 g/6½ oz. wild mushrooms
½ red onion
2 garlic cloves
50 g/⅓ cup shelled pumpkin seeds
sea salt and ground black pepper

SERVES 4

Preheat the oven to 180°C (350°F) Gas 4.

Leave the seeds in the pumpkin, then cut it into 4 wedges and arrange in a roasting dish.

Put 2 tablespoons of the olive oil in a bowl and mix in ½ teaspoon salt, ½ teaspoon pepper, the oregano and cumin. Brush the mixture over the pumpkin wedges.

Roast the pumpkin in the preheated oven for 30–35 minutes. When it is ready, you should be able to slide a sharp knife easily into the flesh.

While the pumpkin is cooking, put the chillies and 250 ml/1 cup water in a saucepan, bring to the boil, then cook for 5 minutes.

Transfer the cooked chillies and their water to a food processor and whizz for 2–3 minutes, then set aside.

Clean the chard, cut off and discard the stems and roughly chop the leaves. Roughly chop the wild mushrooms, onion and garlic.

Put the pumpkin seeds in a dry frying pan over low heat. Stir continuously for 10 minutes, taking care not to let them burn.

Heat the remaining oil in a large saucepan, then fry the mushrooms, onion and garlic over high heat for 1 minute. Add the chard and fry for 2–3 minutes.

Add the puréed chillies and a pinch of salt and pepper and cook for 5 minutes. Remove from the heat, add the pumpkin seeds and mix everything well.

Serve each pumpkin wedge with a portion of vegetables beside it. Eat as it is, or with warm tortillas or bread.

guisado de pescado
cod with plantain & dried fruit

There are numerous fish restaurants in my home town, where the fishermen make a 4-hour journey from the Gulf of Mexico every morning to sell the freshest fish. My mum always made her version of this dish for special occasions such as Christmas and Easter. I love its fruity and aromatic taste which I think surprises a lot of people who are unaware of the variety in Mexican food and its ability to produce beautiful flavours, without necessarily using chillies.

¼ red onion

2 garlic cloves

2 tomatoes, cut into wedges

50 g/3½ tablespoons butter

½ plantain (or banana)

50 g/⅓ cup raisins

100 g/⅔ cup dried apricots

a pinch of ground cinnamon

1 teaspoon brown sugar

a pinch of sea salt

a pinch of ground white pepper

4 skinless cod fillets (or mahi-mahi or halibut), about 500 g/ 1 lb. in total

1 small bunch of coriander/cilantro, finely chopped

SERVING SUGGESTION
basmati rice
green salad

SERVES 4

Thinly slice the onion and garlic, cut the tomatoes into wedges, peel the plantain and slice it on the diagonal.

Melt 20 g/1½ tablespoons of the butter in a saucepan, then fry the onion and garlic over low heat for 1 minute.

Add the tomatoes, plantain, raisins, apricots, cinnamon, sugar, salt and pepper and cook for 2–3 minutes.

Add 250 ml/1 cup water, turn up the heat to high, bring to the boil and boil vigorously for 2 minutes.

Turn the heat down low again and simmer gently for 5–7 minutes until the flavours have combined and you can smell the fragrant aroma of the cinnamon.

Meanwhile, melt the remaining butter in a large frying pan over low heat and add the fish. Season with salt and white pepper and cook for 3 minutes. Flip over, season again and cook for a further 3 minutes. Test that the fish is cooked by inserting a fork gently into the thickest part and twisting slowly. The flesh should begin to separate along its natural lines.

Finally, throw the coriander/cilantro into the sauce and stir.

Gently lay one portion of fish on each plate so as not to break it and cover with the sauce.

SERVING SUGGESTION
Serve with rice and a green salad, if you like.

pescado al ajillo
baked sea bream with garlic butter

2 whole sea bream
(or sea bass or red
snapper), about
500 g/1 lb. each,
scaled and gutted
60 g/4 tablespoons
butter
a pinch of sea salt
1 handful of shredded
Romaine lettuce or
mixed leaves
¼ red onion, very thinly
sliced
2 tomatoes, roughly
chopped
10 garlic cloves, thinly
sliced
1–2 fresh Jalapeños
1 lemon, thinly sliced

CHIPOTLE VINAIGRETTE
175 ml/¾ cup red wine
vinegar
250 ml/1 cup olive oil
1 garlic clove, crushed
1 teaspoon dried
oregano
1 teaspoon Chipotle
paste
a pinch of sea salt
a pinch of ground
black pepper

SERVES 2

Mexico's long coastline means that fresh fish is always plentiful. I know that some people shy away from cooking a whole fish, preferring to use fillets, but cooking it like this really does enhance the flavour and also provides a great wow factor when you bring it to the table. You can fry the fish but I think baking it in the oven gives the best result. I like to serve it with a simple salad and a tasty chipotle vinaigrette. You will have some vinaigrette left over, so keep it to use in a salad another time.

Preheat the oven to 160°C (325°F) Gas 3.

Using a small, sharp knife, cut 3 slits on one side of each fish through to the bone.

Put 10 g/2 teaspoons of the butter in a baking sheet and put in the preheated oven until melted.

Take the baking sheet out of the oven and roll the fish in the melted butter.

Sprinkle the salt all over each fish and lay on the baking sheet. Bake in the middle of the preheated oven for 25–30 minutes. Flip them over halfway through cooking. When the fish is ready, the flesh should be opaque. Return to the oven for a minute or 2 if it is still translucent.

CHIPOTLE VINAIGRETTE
Meanwhile, put the vinegar, olive oil, garlic, oregano, chipotle paste, salt and pepper in a bowl and whisk very well to combine. Set aside.

To make a garlic-jalapeño butter, melt the remaining butter in a saucepan over low heat and fry the garlic and jalapeños for just 2–3 minutes so that they infuse the butter but don't have time to burn.

Toss the lettuce, onion and tomatoes together with 2 tablespoons of the chipotle vinaigrette and set aside.

Place each fish, slit side up, on a plate and pour the garlic-jalapeño butter over the slits. Serve with the salad and lemon slices for squeezing over the fish.

enfrijoladas
corn tortillas dipped in black bean sauce
with queso fresco

This hearty and simple dish was typically cooked in the fields to eat during the harvest, and the tradition continues to this day. The beans and corn were often grown in fields together, while all the other ingredients were available close at hand so that the workers could literally pick the avocado leaves straight from a nearby tree and throw them in. As a child I went to the fields to help my family collect the beans and corn at harvest time and I always looked forward to this as my reward.

1 quantity cooked black (turtle) beans from Frijoles Negros con Hojas de Aguacate (page 88)
1 teaspoon ground avocado leaves
1 teaspoon sea salt
2 tablespoons vegetable oil, plus 250 ml/1 cup (optional)
20 x 15-cm/6-in. corn tortillas

TO SERVE
200 g/2 cups crumbled queso fresco, feta or cheddar cheese
¼ onion, halved and very thinly sliced

SERVES 4

Put the cooked beans, avocado leaves and salt in a food processor and whizz for 3 minutes.

Heat the 2 tablespoons of oil in a saucepan over medium heat, then fry the puréed beans for 7–8 minutes until piping hot throughout. They should be quite runny, so you may need to add a little extra water.

To fry the tortillas, heat the 250 ml/ 2 cups vegetable oil in a large pan over medium heat. Using tongs, dip each tortilla into the hot oil for a few seconds. Allow to drain on kitchen paper/paper towels. If you don't want to use the oil, you can heat them in a dry frying pan over high heat for about 10 seconds on each side.

Using tongs again, dip each softened tortilla into the puréed beans until well coated, then fold into quarters.

TO SERVE
Arrange 5 overlapping tortillas on each plate and sprinkle the cheese and onion over the top.

*

AVOCADO LEAVES have a subtle aniseed flavour. Outside Mexico, they are available dried and whole (in which case they can be used to impart their flavour to dishes during cooking and then discarded at the end before serving), or dried and ground.

Only the leaves from the Mexican variety of the avocado are edible and they are used in a wide range of dishes. If you can't find avocado leaves then star anise is a decent substitute. Crush one "flower" to powder for every teaspoon of avocado leaves and follow the recipe as normal.

para
acompañar

SIDE DISHES

frijoles negros con hojas de aguacate
refried black beans with avocado leaves

175 g/1 cup dried black (turtle) beans
1 tablespoon vegetable oil
¼ onion, finely chopped
1 garlic clove, finely chopped
1 teaspoon ground avocado leaves
a pinch of sea salt

SERVES 4–6

Put the dried beans and 2 litres/8 cups water in a deep saucepan. Bring to the boil, then turn the heat down to low, partially cover and simmer gently for 2 hours. Check every 30 minutes to be sure there is still enough water and stir so that the beans don't stick to the bottom.

After 2 hours, heat the oil in a large saucepan over medium heat and fry the onion, garlic and avocado leaves for 1 minute.

Add the beans and their cooking water and cook until they start to boil, then turn the heat down to low, add the salt and cook for 10 minutes, crushing the beans regularly with a potato masher. Taste and add more salt if required.

frijoles negros con chorizo
refried black beans with chorizo

1 quantity cooked black (turtle) beans from recipe above
1 teaspoon vegetable oil
100 g/3½ oz. chorizo, thinly sliced
sea salt
200 g/2 cups crumbled feta cheese

SERVES 4–6

Follow the first paragraph from the recipe above and then continue here.

Put the oil in a non-stick frying pan over medium heat – you only need a very small amount because the chorizo will release some of its own oils on cooking.

Add the chorizo and fry for about 1–2 minutes, then remove half the chorizo from the pan and set aside.

Add the beans and their cooking water to the pan and cook until they start to boil, then turn the heat down to low and cook for 10 minutes, crushing the beans and chorizo regularly with a potato masher. This will blend the flavours beautifully. Taste and add salt if required.

Sprinkle the reserved chorizo and some feta over the top to serve.

Black turtle beans are a staple of Mexican cuisine. Back home, once the beans have been boiled but before we add other ingredients, the adults set aside some of the broth, add pieces of tortilla and give it to young children. The broth is rich in iron and introduces them them to the flavour of the beans.

frijoles refritos con paprika
refried pinto beans with paprika

You will be hard pressed to find a restaurant in Mexico that does not serve its own version of this classic. This take is very popular with our customers.

175 g/1 cup dried pinto beans

½ teaspoon sea salt

1 tablespoon vegetable oil

¼ onion, finely chopped

1 garlic clove, crushed

2 teaspoons paprika

SERVES 4

Put the dried beans and 1.5 litres/ 6 cups water in a saucepan. Bring to the boil, then turn the heat down to low, partially cover and simmer gently for 2–2½ hours. Add a little more water if necessary. You should be able to crush the beans easily.

Heat the oil in a large saucepan over medium heat and fry the onion and garlic for a few seconds.

Add the beans, their cooking water and the paprika and cook for 10 minutes over medium-low heat, mashing continuously with a potato masher. Add a little extra boiling water if dry, and taste and add more salt if required.

frijoles del norte
northern–style refried pinto beans

This is for meat lovers — using sausages, frankfurters and pancetta. It is my own rich and hearty take on the popular "frijoles charros", or cowboy beans.

1 quantity cooked pinto beans from recipe above

100 g/3½ oz. good pork sausages

3 frankfurters

100 g/3½ oz. pork belly or pancetta

¼ onion

2 tomatoes

1 small bunch of coriander/cilantro

1 tablespoon vegetable oil

1 teaspoon sea salt

SERVES 4

Follow the first paragraph from the recipe above and then continue here.

Cut the sausages and frankfurters into small, equal chunks. Finely chop the pork belly or pancetta, onion, tomatoes and coriander/cilantro.

Put the oil in a saucepan over medium-high heat and fry the pork belly or pancetta for 5–7 minutes, stirring regularly, until browned. Add the sausages and fry for 5 minutes or until well done. It is important that these ingredients are cooked through.

Add the onion and frankfurters and fry for 1 minute.

Add the salt and the beans, together with their cooking water, bring to the boil and cook for 2 minutes.

Turn the heat down to low, add the tomatoes and coriander and simmer for 10 minutes.

When ready, the liquid should have a slightly creamy consistency. Add a little extra boiling water if dry, and taste and add more salt if required.

chiles toreados
sautéed onions with chillies

This simple side dish can be used to add fire to any meal. "Toreados" comes from the word "torear", meaning to bull fight. Here it describes the reaction that happens when you sauté chillies, thereby increasing their spicy kick.

10–15 fresh Jalapeños or Chiles de Arbol/ Thai green chillies
1 onion
1 tablespoon olive oil
1 lime or lemon, cut into wedges
2 pinches of sea salt

SERVES 6–8

Cut any particularly large chillies in half lengthways but otherwise leave them whole.

Thinly slice the onion.

Heat the oil in a saucepan and fry the chillies and onion for 2–3 minutes.

Remove from the heat and squeeze the lime or lemon into the pan.

Season with the salt and mix together well. Taste and add more salt if required.

＊

JALAPEÑOS are perfect for adding to Mexican dishes or scattering over pizzas. However, buy them fresh and you will better appreciate their fiery flavour. They are small and plump with a thick flesh and you will usually find them green, although if left to ripen on the plant, they turn red. They are wonderful thrown into potent salsas, like the Salsa Diabla on page 103.

arroz con cilantro
coriander–lime rice

Rice forms the foundation of most Mexican meals so it's particularly important to give it proper care and attention and not serve it in the same plain way every time. Follow this recipe and you will get beautiful, fluffy rice with fresh lime and coriander and earthiness from the white pepper.

2 tablespoons vegetable oil
200 g/1 cup basmati rice
¼ onion, finely chopped
a pinch of sea salt
a pinch of ground white pepper
1 medium bunch of coriander/cilantro, finely chopped
1 tablespoon lime juice

SERVES 2

Heat the oil in a deep saucepan, then fry the rice, onion, salt and pepper over low heat for 2–3 minutes, stirring continuously.

Add 500 ml/2 cups water, cover with a lid and cook for about 8–10 minutes or according to the pack instructions. After it has been boiling for about 5 minutes, carefully taste the cooking water – this will give you a good idea of what your rice will taste like, so add more seasoning now if necessary.

Stir in the coriander/cilantro and lime juice just before serving.

arroz a la jardinera
sautéed rice with spring veg

This rice dish is supposed to be based on whatever you have in the garden but ultimately, it is about throwing in as many and as varied vegetables you like to make a full, flavourful and tasty rice dish.

¼ red onion
2 garlic cloves
2 carrots
2 tablespoons vegetable oil
400 g/2 cups basmati rice
100 g/3½ oz. wild or oyster mushrooms
1 teaspoon sea salt
¼ teaspoon ground white pepper
1 vegetable stock cube
100 g/3½ oz. baby corn
100 g/1 cup mangetout/snow peas
4 green chillies

SERVES 4

Thinly slice the onion and garlic. Cut the carrots into matchsticks.

Heat the oil in a large saucepan over medium heat, then fry the rice, onion, garlic, mushrooms salt and pepper for 3–5 minutes.

Dissolve the stock cube in 1 litre/4 cups boiling water and add to the pan with the carrots, baby corn, mangetout/snow peas and chillies. Boil for about 2 minutes, then turn down the heat to low, cover with a lid and simmer gently for 10 minutes or according to the pack instructions.

tesmole de ejotes
spicy green bean stew

As far as I'm aware, this is a dish that is unique to the village I come from. Spicy green beans might be something you are more used to seeing on Chinese restaurant menus but I'm sure you'll love this Mexican version.

3 tomatoes
½ onion, peeled
2 garlic cloves, peeled and slightly bruised
1 tablespoon paprika
1 teaspoon dried epazote
3–5 dried Chiles de Arbol (or similar hot dried chilli)
½ teaspoon sea salt
2½ tablespoons vegetable oil
200 g/6½ oz. green beans, topped and tailed
1 tablespoon masa harina or plain/all-purpose flour
125 ml/½ cup warm water

SERVES 4

Preheat the oven to 180°C (350°F) Gas 4.

Put the tomatoes, onion and garlic in a roasting dish and roast in the preheated oven for 20–25 minutes, turning every 8 minutes or so. Once lightly charred all over, remove from the oven and allow to cool for a few minutes.

Put the roasted ingredients in a food processor or blender with 2 litres/8 cups water, the paprika, epazote, chillies and salt. Whizz for 2 minutes.

Heat 2 tablespoons of the oil in a saucepan over medium heat.

Strain the blended ingredients through a sieve/strainer into the pan of oil, pressing the mixture through with the back of a large spoon. Bring to the boil and cook for 5 minutes.

Heat the remaining oil in a separate pan, then fry the beans for 1 minute. Transfer the beans to the sauce and simmer gently for 5 minutes.

Mix the masa harina or flour into the warm water until combined, then add to the sauce and simmer for about 5–7 minutes.

EPAZOTE is an ancient Mexican herb used in cooking since the time of the Aztecs. With a potent smell and taste, it is regularly used in Mexican dishes for its flavour but also to offset the negative digestive side effects of eating beans! Historically, it was used as medicine to counteract this very unwanted side effect, but is in fact poisonous when eaten in very large doses.

Epazote leaves for cooking are most easily found dried and crushed (see page 140). Dried oregano can be used as a good substitute to epazote as it has a similar flavour, especially once cooked.

salsas

SALSAS

Salsa brava is a pretty fiery salsa; it is the "hot" option at Benito's Hat. If you want to go all the way to the limit, there is the Salsa Diabla on page 103 but this one still packs a good punch. The roasted tomatoes give it great depth as well as a creamy texture. If you find that you are getting heat but no flavour, that means the tomatoes, onions and garlic have not blackened enough.

"fierce" salsa

4 tomatoes

3 Habaneros or Scotch Bonnet chillies, stalks removed

½ onion, roughly chopped

4 garlic cloves, peeled

2 tablespoons vegetable oil

4 tablespoons crushed dried chillies

sea salt

MAKES A BOWLFUL

Preheat the oven to 180°C (350°F) Gas 4.

Put the tomatoes, whole chillies, onion and garlic in a roasting dish and roast in the preheated oven for about 15–20 minutes or until evenly blackened, turning occasionally with metal tongs. Remove from the oven and allow to cool for 10 minutes.

Heat the oil in a saucepan for 1 minute. Remove from the heat, add the crushed chillies and stir well.

With a molcajete (see page 104) or pestle and mortar, crush the roasted chillies, onion and garlic very well for about 3 minutes.

Add the chilli oil and crush again for 3 minutes.

Add the roasted tomatoes and pound well for another 2 minutes, then mix in 175 ml/⅔ cup water and a couple of pinches of salt. Continue to pound until all the ingredients are very well blended.

salsa de aguacate avocado salsa

The avocado here gives this medium-spiced salsa a wonderfully creamy texture that contrasts beautifully with the tang of the tomatillos and the heat of the chillies. It goes very well with the Barbacoa de Cordero (page 70).

1–2 fresh green chillies, stalks removed

2 garlic cloves, peeled

6–8 fresh tomatillos, husks removed

3 tablespoons chopped coriander/cilantro

1 big tablespoon very finely chopped onion

2 ripe avocados, pitted and peeled

a pinch of sea salt

MAKES A BOWLFUL

Preheat the oven to 200°C (400°F) Gas 6.

Put the chillies, garlic and tomatillos on a baking sheet and roast in the preheated oven for 15–20 minutes or until slightly charred.

Cut the chillies in half and scrape out the seeds (or leave them in if you want to take it up a notch!) Put in a food processor with all the other ingredients and whizz for 2 minutes. Add a little water or salt, if required.

* AVOCADOS are native to central Mexico. Now one of the most traded tropical fruits in the world, Mexico remains the biggest producer. Anyone who is a fan of this rich, creamy fruit (mostly but not exclusively used in savoury dishes) has tried guacamole or a variation at least once and fallen in love with its fresh, zingy flavour.

salsa diabla "she-devil" salsa

There is a clue in the title of this very spicy salsa – in Spanish, "diabla" means "she-devil" and this salsa doesn't pull any punches. I recommend it only to those who can take very hot food and, even then, only eat it in small quantities.

10 extra-hot dried chillies

2 Habaneros or Scotch Bonnet chillies

3 fresh green Jalapeños

1 tablespoon vegetable oil

2 tomatoes

1 garlic clove, peeled

a pinch of dried oregano

a pinch of sea salt

MAKES A BOWLFUL

Cut the stalks off all the chillies and roughly chop the tomatoes.

Put the oil in a saucepan over medium heat and add the whole chillies, tomatoes and garlic. Cover with a lid and cook for about 8–10 minutes. Stir occasionally so that the ingredients are evenly cooked but are not burning.

Remove from the heat and allow to cool for 10 minutes.

Put the cooled ingredients, oregano, salt and 175 ml/⅔ cup water in a food processor and whizz for 2 minutes or until well blended.

salsa borracha
"drunken" salsa

1 Habanero, stalk
  removed
2 garlic cloves, peeled
3–4 tomatoes
60 ml/¼ cup beer,
  preferably a dark,
  Munich-style beer
  like Negra Modelo,
  but any lager works
  well
½ teaspoon rock salt
chopped coriander/
cilantro (optional)

MAKES A BOWLFUL

Preheat the oven to 200°C (400°F) Gas 6.

Put the chilli, garlic and tomatoes on a baking sheet and roast in the preheated oven for 15–20 minutes or until charred. The chilli and garlic may need less time than the tomatoes, so remove them from the baking sheet early if necessary.

Using a molcajete (see below) or pestle and mortar, pound the chilli, garlic and salt into a paste. Add the tomatoes and pound until well mixed. Add the beer and mix again.

Add more salt to taste, if required. Stir in the chopped coriander/cilantro, if using.

salsa verde
roasted tomatillo salsa

1–2 fresh green chillies,
  stalks removed
2 garlic cloves, peeled
2–3 fresh tomatillos,
  husks removed (or
  canned tomatillos)
3 tablespoons chopped
  coriander/cilantro
¼ chopped onion
1 teaspoon rock salt

MAKES A BOWLFUL

Preheat the oven to 200°C (400°F) Gas 6.

Put the chillies, garlic and tomatillos on a baking sheet and roast in the preheated oven for 20 minutes or until charred. If using canned tomatillos, don't roast them.

Halve the chillies and scoop out the seeds. Using a molcajete or pestle and mortar, pound the chillies, garlic and salt into a paste. Add the tomatillos and pound until well mixed. Add the coriander/cilantro and onion and stir with a spoon. Add a little water or salt, if required.

* **TOMATILLOS** are usually available during the summer from various online sellers and canned ones are available all year round. They are worth seeking out as they provide a delicious, unique, tangy flavour that sets them apart from their cousins the tomatoes. Their tartness is very specific to Mexican cooking but they are sure to win over anyone trying them for the first time.

MOLCAJETES are similar to pestles and mortars but are made from volcanic rock. To make a salsa in a molcajete is very rewarding and the result is better than when a food processor is used. For centuries, the molcajete has been used to make the wonderful salsas that I am proud to continue making today.

guacamole guacamole

Guacamole is the one of the most widely known side dishes in Mexican cooking outside of Mexico. It was made as early as the 16th century by the Aztec people. There are numerous recipes throughout Mexico but for me the recipe below allows the flavour and texture of the avocado to shine through.

2–3 avocados
1 medium bunch of
**   coriander/cilantro**
1 tomato
a pinch of sea salt
a pinch of ground
**   white pepper**

MAKES A BOWLFUL

Pit and peel the avocados. Scoop the flesh out into a bowl. Finely chop the coriander/cilantro and add to the bowl with the salt and pepper. Roughly mash with a fork. Finely chop the tomatoes and stir into the guacamole.

pico de gallo fresh tomato salsa

When these fresh, simple ingredients are combined together, they produce a wonderful salsa bursting with flavour. Like other Mexican salsas, there are many variations, such as adding lime juice and fresh chillies. Because it's not spicy, it can be enjoyed by my kids as well.

4 tomatoes
¼ onion
1 medium bunch of
**   coriander/cilantro**
¼ teaspoon sea salt

MAKES A BOWLFUL

Finely chop the tomatoes, onion and coriander/cilantro and put in a bowl. Add the salt and mix well.

Next time you make this mild salsa, adjust the proportions according to your taste.

*CORIANDER/CILANTRO has such a distinctive, pungent taste that it invokes very strong opinions – both positive and negative! Those who like it rave about the fresh, clean fragrance it adds to dishes, especially spicy ones. Add it at the end of a recipe so that its flavour isn't lost in cooking. This is a herb to enjoy raw and zingy.

postres

DESSERTS

pan de muerto de mi abuela
"Day of the Dead" bread

This is dedicated to my grandmother Hermelinda, for whom I would wait excitedly each year on the Day of the Dead to make this bread. It is traditionally flavoured with almonds and orange zest and sprinkled with sesame seeds. You really must knead the dough well so as to create bubbles and then the bread can be shaped into a variety of shapes — here we have chosen the traditional skull and crossbones.

560 g/4½ cups plain/
   all-purpose flour
3 tablespoons warm
   water
2 teaspoons active dry
   yeast
1 medium egg
7 medium egg yolks
grated zest of 2 oranges
4 tablespoons orange
   juice
1 teaspoon cocoa
   powder
1 teaspoon ground
   cinnamon
200 g/1 cup sugar
1 tablespoon pure
   vanilla extract
60 ml/¼ cup milk
80 g/½ cup ground
   almonds
a pinch of salt
100 g/6½ tablespoons
   salted butter, melted
sesame seeds,
   to sprinkle

baking sheet, lined with
   parchment paper

MAKES 6

Put 3 tablespoons of the flour, the warm water and the yeast in a small mixing bowl. Mix together, cover and allow to stand for 20 minutes.

Put the whole egg and 5 of the egg yolks, the orange zest and juice, cocoa, cinnamon, sugar, vanilla, milk, ground almonds and salt in a bowl and mix well. Add the melted butter and mix well.

Put the remaining flour in a large mixing bowl and make a well in the middle. Add the wet mixture and mix well with a spatula.

Add the rested yeast mixture and knead for about 5 minutes, bringing the mixture from the outside towards the middle.

Cover the bowl with a tea towel and allow to rise for at least 1 hour at room temperature.

When you are ready to shape the bread, preheat the oven to 160°C (325°F) Gas 3.

Turn the dough out onto the work surface. Shape it into a large sausage, then slice it into 4 equal

pieces. Set one piece aside: slice each of the remaining pieces in half. Roll each of these 6 pieces into a tight ball. Place on the prepared baking sheet, leaving about 5 cm/ 2 inches between the balls.

From the large piece of dough you set aside, pinch off 6 little pieces: roll them into tight balls about the size of marbles. Roll the remaining dough into a rope and cut it into 12 equal pieces. Open out the fingers of one hand and roll them over each short rope of dough until it looks like a little femur bone.

Gently stretch each "bone" across a ball of dough on the baking sheet and place another at right angles to make a cross shape. Place a dough "marble" where the "bones" cross.

Mix the remaining egg yolks with a few drops of water and brush this over the breads, to glaze. Sprinkle some sesame seeds on top.

Bake in the preheated oven for about 25 minutes or until golden brown, turning the baking sheet halfway through.

pastel de tres leches
three-milk cake

Pastel de tres leches is made using 3 types of milk — sweetened condensed, evaporated and whole milk. The cake is an intriguing creation, managing to be both rich and light at the same time. The creamy syrup that is poured over contrasts beautifully with the fluffy texture of the cake. It is a delicacy that is traditionally served at special occasions such as weddings and christenings — but at Benito's Hat, it's served every day of the week!

3 medium eggs, separated
1 tablespoon pure vanilla extract
200 g/1 cup (caster) sugar
130 g/1 cup self-raising flour
2 teaspoons baking powder
250 ml/1 cup evaporated milk
250 ml/1 cup sweetened condensed milk
250 ml/1 cup milk

TO SERVE
250 ml/1 cup double/ heavy cream
strawberries

20-cm/8-in. springform cake pan, greased and dusted with flour

SERVES 6

Preheat the oven to 150°C (300°F) Gas 2.

Put the egg whites in a mixing bowl and mix gently with a balloon whisk for 1–2 minutes – do not over-whisk or allow to become frothy.

Add the egg yolks and mix for about 1 minute.

Whisking continuously, gradually add the vanilla, sugar, flour and baking powder in this order, allowing 1 minute between each addition.

Pour the mixture into the prepared cake pan and bake on the middle shelf of the preheated oven for 35 minutes. When it is ready, a skewer inserted in the middle of the cake should come out clean.

Remove from the oven and allow to cool in the pan for 30 minutes.

Pour the 3 types of milk into a blender and whizz for 2 minutes.

Once the cake has cooled, tip it out of the pan and onto a serving dish. Prick holes all over the top of the cake with a fork.

Pour the milk mixture over the cake and allow it to seep in for 10 minutes. It will look like you have far too much liquid, but don't worry as the cake will quickly soak it up.

TO SERVE
When you are ready to serve the cake, put the cream in a bowl and whip with a balloon whisk or electric whisk until soft peaks form.

Using a spatula, spread the cream over the top of the cake, leaving a border around the edge. Decorate with the strawberries.

buñuelos
cinnamon fritters with ice cream

When we opened Benito's Hat in 2008, we didn't have any desserts on the menu. After a few months, a customer asked for something sweet after her meal and I wanted to make something to please her. I had to use ingredients that we had to hand in the kitchen, so I created this dish and other customers in the restaurant were soon asking for it too. We haven't looked back since.

4 flour tortillas
250 ml/1 cup vegetable
    oil
2 tablespoons (caster)
    sugar
1 teaspoon ground
    cinnamon

TO SERVE
good-quality vanilla
    ice cream
ground cinnamon
strawberries

SERVES 2

Cut the tortillas into strips about 2 cm/¾ inches wide.

Pour the vegetable oil into a saucepan over medium heat and leave until the oil is very hot but not smoking.

Carefully drop in the tortilla strips in batches and fry for 1 minute or until they are light brown, turning the strips gently and often with tongs to prevent them from burning.

Using the tongs or a slotted spoon, remove the strips from the pan and allow to drain on kitchen paper/paper towels. Repeat the process until all the strips have been fried.

Mix the sugar and cinnamon.

Place the tortilla strips in a large bowl and add the cinnamon-sugar. Toss together until well coated.

TO SERVE
Scoop some ice cream into 2 bowls or cocktail glasses, stand the tortilla strips around the edge and dust cinnamon over the top. Serve with a strawberry or 2.

*

CINNAMON has the kind of warm, sweet aroma that makes it instantly recognisable in both sweet and savoury dishes. Available to buy in short sticks or quills, or ready ground in jars, you'll find that the strength of its aroma is always better in stick form. It makes an irresistible addition to desserts and drinks.

flan casero
homemade flan

Flan is a traditional Mexican dessert but it is also very similar to a dessert that is well known and loved in France and worldwide – crème caramel. As always, there are many different versions of Mexican flan and this is the one we have adapted for Benito's Hat by adding a gentle hint of vanilla.

200 g/1 cup (caster) sugar
410-g/14.5 oz. can of evaporated milk
397-g/14-oz. can of sweetened condensed milk
4 medium eggs
2 tablespoons pure vanilla extract

TO SERVE
raspberries

25 x 25-cm/10 x 10-in. baking dish
fluted, round cookie cutter

SERVES 6

Preheat the oven to 160°C (325°F) Gas 3.

Put the sugar in a saucepan over medium heat and cook for about 5 minutes, stirring constantly, until the mixture turns golden brown. Don't worry when the sugar starts to stick to the spoon – just keep going and it will turn out right! When you have the right colour, immediately remove from the heat.

Pour the caramelized sugar into the baking dish. Swirl it around the dish until it covers the base evenly.

Put the evaporated milk, condensed milk, eggs and vanilla extract in a mixing bowl and whisk with an electric whisk on a low setting for 20–30 seconds. Pour the mixture over the caramelized sugar in the baking dish.

Boil a full kettle of water.

Put the baking dish in the middle of a larger roasting pan. Pour the boiled water into the roasting pan until it reaches halfway up the sides of the baking dish – this is a bain marie and will allow the flan to bake slowly and evenly. The resulting steam will also prevent a crust from forming on top of the flan.

Put the roasting pan on the middle shelf of the preheated oven and bake for 1 hour and 15 minutes.

Remove the flan from the oven and allow it to cool for 1 hour.

TO SERVE
Carefully run a knife around the edge of the flan to loosen it from the sides of the baking dish. Place a large plate face down over the baking dish. Carefully flip both over, then lay on a surface. Ease off the baking dish.

Using the cookie cutter, stamp out as many discs as possible from the flan. Slide a spatula underneath each disc and transfer to individual plates. Alternatively, cut the flan into 6 equal portions.

Pour some of the caramelized liquid from the baking dish on top of each flan and serve with raspberries.

burrito de manzana
caramelized apple burrito

I love this dish for its simplicity. My time living in the US taught me a love for apple pie and this takes the same simple principle that stewed, spiced apples in a crispy casing are something beautiful. If you feel you need a break from tortillas, you can always make the filling as per the recipe and encase them in pastry.

1 tablespoon (caster) sugar
2 teaspoons ground cinnamon
500 g/1 lb. apples
50 ml/3 tablespoons agave syrup
4 x 20-cm/8-in. flour tortilla
vegetable oil, for frying

TO SERVE
300 ml/1¼ cups double/ heavy cream
4 scoops of good-quality vanilla ice cream
mint, to garnish

cocktail sticks/ toothpicks

SERVES 4

Mix the sugar and half the cinnamon and set aside.

Peel and core the apples and cut into small chunks.

Put the agave syrup in a small saucepan over medium heat, add the apple chunks and remaining cinnamon and cook for 7–10 minutes or until the apples have softened and caramelized.

Divide the apple mixture into 4 equal portions.

Lay a tortilla on a surface and place a portion of the apple mixture in the middle. Fold the right and left sides of the tortilla over the filling so that they overlap and the tortilla is one third of its original width. Fold the top and bottom of the tortilla to the middle so that one side covers the other and you have a shape like a burrito. Secure the tortilla with cocktail sticks/toothpicks to ensure that the filling does not spill out.

Repeat this process with the remaining tortillas and portions of apple mixture.

Pour some vegetable oil into a deep frying pan until it comes 2 cm/¾ inch up the side of the pan. Set over medium heat and leave until the oil is very hot but not smoking.

Carefully drop in one burrito at a time and fry until golden brown, turning it gently and occasionally with tongs to prevent it from burning.

Using the tongs or a slotted spoon, remove the burrito from the pan and allow to drain on kitchen paper/ paper towels. Repeat the process until all the burritos have been fried.

Once the burritos are cool enough to handle, remove the sticks.

TO SERVE
Put the cream in a bowl and whip with a balloon whisk or electric whisk until soft peaks form.

Serve each burrito with a scoop of vanilla ice cream, a generous dusting of the cinnamon and sugar mixture, a good dollop of whipped cream and a mint-leaf garnish.

pastel de galletas con piña
pineapple layered cookie cake

This cake is made by my aunt and cousins for all the family gatherings in our village. I am certain our parties would be much less well attended if this cake wasn't guaranteed to be there! It has become a favourite dessert for me, my wife and children with the twist that I have introduced by incorporating my dad's favourite coffee. The coffee cuts through the sweetness of the pineapple for a really beautiful combination of flavours.

1 pineapple
250 ml/1 cup evaporated milk
250 ml/1 cup sweetened condensed milk
100 g/6 tablespoons cream cheese
100 ml/6 tablespoons lime juice
300 g/10 oz. Rich Tea biscuits or Graham crackers
250 ml/1 cup Cafe de Don Felipe (page 131)

20 x 20-cm/8 x 8-in. square or round baking pan
round cookie cutter

SERVES 6

Before peeling the pineapple, cut off and discard the ends. Cut one round about 1 cm/½ inch thick, then chop into triangular strips around the tough core. Discard the core and set the strips aside. Peel the rest of the pineapple and chop it into small chunks, discarding the core.

Put the evaporated milk, condensed milk and cream cheese in a blender and whizz for 1 minute. Slowly add the lime juice and whizz for 1 minute or until the mixture is thick.

Put the biscuits or crackers in a shallow bowl with the Cafe de Don Felipe and allow to soak for up to 1 minute or until the coffee has been absorbed. Do not allow to soak for too long otherwise the biscuits/crackers will break.

Spread a layer of the milk mixture into the baking pan. Add a layer of soaked biscuits, then scatter a little of the pineapple over the top. You need about 250 g/9 oz. pineapple here so, depending on the size of your fruit, you may have a bit left over to serve on the side.

Repeat this process until you have used up all the ingredients, ensuring that you finish with a layer of the milk mixture.

Cover the baking tray with clingfilm/plastic wrap and freeze for 30 minutes or until it solidifies and has a texture like soft ice cream. Do not freeze for longer, as ice will start to form in the pineapple, which spoils the flavour.

Meanwhile, heat a ridged stovetop grill pan over medium heat. Place the reserved pineapple strips on the pan and grill for 2–3 minutes on each side. You want to get quite clear char marks and it will give the pineapple a delicious caramelized flavour.

Using the cookie cutter, stamp out as many discs as possible from the cake. Slide a spatula underneath each disc and transfer to individual plates. Alternatively, cut the cake into 6 equal portions. Lay a piece of grilled pineapple on each serving.

bebidas

DRINKS

agua de piña con apio
pineapple & celery water

The pineapple and celery here complement each other wonderfully to make a drink that is refreshing, healthy and very popular in Mexican markets.

1 small pineapple or 500 g/1 lb. pineapple chunks
300 g/10 oz. celery
2½ tablespoons (caster) sugar
1 tablespoon lime juice

SERVES 4

Peel, core and chop the pineapple.

Remove the leaves and some of the strands from the celery, then chop.

Put all the ingredients and 750 ml/3 cups water in a blender and whizz for 3 minutes.

Strain the liquid through a sieve/strainer and, using a large spoon, press as much of the pulp through the sieve as possible. Discard any remaining pulp.

Serve chilled over ice.

agua de sandía
watermelon water

Watermelons are abundant throughout Mexico. Therefore, this drink has become common everywhere you go. It's easy to make and is very refreshing but, to serve in colder countries, wait until the summer when watermelons start to appear on greengrocers' shelves.

½ medium watermelon (about 1.2 kg/3 lbs.)
2 tablespoons (caster) sugar
1 tablespoon lime juice

SERVES 4

Cut the watermelon into large slices and remove the seeds using a fork.

Scoop the watermelon flesh into a blender and add the sugar, lime juice and 250 ml/1 cup water. Whizz for 2 minutes.

Serve chilled over ice.

A simple, pressed lime and lemon drink will refresh you any day. Our version has become extremely popular at Benito's Hat, where we squeeze boxes and boxes of fresh limes every day. Using agave syrup instead of sugar gives an extra quality to the flavour but you can use caster/superfine sugar if you prefer.

horchata milkshake with cinnamon & rice

This Mexican milkshake has a wonderful, delicate cinnamon flavour. Traditionally, a "molino de mano" is used to grind the rice by hand, however, here we have used a standard blender which does the job well.

180 g/1 cup white rice

½ teaspoon ground cinnamon, plus extra to dust

2 tablespoons (caster) sugar

625 ml/2½ cups whole milk

125 ml/½ cup sweetened condensed milk

SERVES 4

Put the rice, cinnamon, sugar and 250 ml/1 cup water in a blender and whizz until completely smooth, which may take as long as 7–8 minutes.

Add 500 ml/2 cups water, the whole milk and condensed milk to the blender and whizz for 1–2 minutes.

Strain the liquid through a sieve/strainer.

Serve over ice and dust some cinnamon on top.

agua de limón limeade

2 tablespoons agave syrup or caster/ superfine sugar (dissolved in a little hot water)

2 lemons

4 limes

SERVES 4

Pour 1 litre/4 cups water in a jug/pitcher, add the agave syrup and mix well.

Wash the lemons and limes, cut them in half and squeeze the juice into the jug/pitcher.

Cut half the squeezed lemons and limes in half again and add them to the jug/pitcher.

Serve over ice.

agua de flor de jamaica
hibiscus flower water

This is made using the calyces of the hibiscus flower, which gives it a wonderful, deep red colour. It is a very refreshing drink and tastes particularly good straight out of the fridge on a hot day!

20 g/¾ oz. dried
   hibiscus calyces or
   flor de Jamaica
60 g/⅓ cup (caster)
   sugar

SERVES 4

Put the flowers, sugar and 2 litres/4 cups water in a large saucepan over high heat and bring to the boil.

Boil for 5–7 minutes. Remove from the heat and allow to cool for 1 hour.

Strain the liquid through a sieve/strainer.

Serve chilled over ice.

agua de tamarindo
tamarind water

Tamarind is an exotic fruit — uncommon in the UK but widely used in Mexico and the States, as well as in Africa and India. In Mexico it is particularly popular in one of the many varieties of "aguas frescas" (literally meaning "fresh waters") and for flavouring candy.

200 g/1⅓ cups tamarind
   pulp and seeds
3–3½ tablespoons
   caster/superfine
   sugar

SERVES 4

Pour 1.5 litres/6 cups water, the tamarind pulp and seeds and sugar in a large saucepan and bring to the boil. Cover with a lid and simmer over low heat for 10 minutes. Remove from the heat and allow to cool for at least 1 hour.

Just before serving, strain the liquid through a sieve/strainer. Don't do this until you are ready to serve the drink, as the pulp and seeds continue to infuse the water after cooking.

Serve chilled over ice.

TAMARIND fruits are native to eastern Africa. They grow as large pods containing shiny seeds and a sticky brown pulp. The overwhelming flavour of tamarind is sourness and it is popular in Indian, Middle Eastern and Mexican cooking. You can buy dried tamarind pods, or jars and cans of the pulp.

HIBISCUS is often consumed as tea by stewing the calyces of the flowers to produce a drink with a tart flavour similar to cranberries. Its unique taste and the deep red colour it imparts makes it a popular ingredient in Mexican "aguas frescas".

chocolate caliente
hot chocolate

30 g/1 oz. 100% dark chocolate, very finely chopped

500 ml/2 cups whole milk

2 tablespoons (caster) sugar

½ teaspoon ground cinnamon

TO SERVE
2 cinnamon sticks

SERVES 2

Put all the ingredients in a medium saucepan over high heat. Heat, stirring constantly with a whisk, until the mixture comes to the boil.

Immediately remove from the heat and whisk vigorously for 1 minute.

Divide between 2 cups and pop a cinnamon stick in each one.

This recipe is dedicated to my late dad because it was his favourite way of serving coffee. Including this recipe in this book is very emotional for me, as it is a way of feeling that my dad is part of this experience. When I was little, the tradition was for the woman to make the coffee for her man, but these days it is me who makes this for my wife.

cafe de don felipe
Felipe's cinnamon coffee

2 cinnamon sticks, broken into pieces

2½ tablespoons brown sugar

2 tablespoons fresh ground coffee

SERVES 4

Put 1 litre/4 cups water, the sugar and cinnamon into a large saucepan over high heat. Bring to the boil, then boil for 3 minutes.

Remove from the heat and add the coffee. Allow to infuse for 5 minutes.

Using a fine sieve/strainer, drain the coffee, then serve straightaway while it is good and hot.

atole de avena
oatmeal & cinnamon drink

Atole de avena is a hot, thick, cinnamon-flavoured drink. The "atole" part is the traditional Mexican milk-based drink that is thickened with a grain such as oatmeal or rice. Chocolate is another popular version (known as "champurrado") but here we have gone for cinnamon. I recommend using agave syrup to sweeten the drink because it has a more natural flavour than sugar. I have a slight intolerance to sugar so I like to use agave syrup or honey in my drinks and, as agave syrup is a natural sweetener, it has none of the bitter aftertaste associated with artificial sweeteners.

120 g/1 cup oatmeal
750 ml/3 cups whole milk
100 g/²⁄₃ cup raisins
2 cinnamon sticks, broken into big pieces
5 tablespoons agave syrup

SERVES 4–6

Put the oatmeal and 1 litre/4 cups water in a large saucepan over medium heat and bring to the boil.

Turn the heat down to low and cook for 2–3 minutes, stirring continuously, until the oatmeal has thickened and absorbed all the water.

Add the milk, raisins, cinnamon and agave syrup and bring to the boil, stirring continuously.

Reduce the heat to low and simmer very gently for 1 minute to allow it to thicken slightly.

Divide the drink between 4–6 cups, making sure that each cup gets some raisins.

*

AGAVE SYRUP OR NECTAR is a syrup extracted mostly from the blue agave plant that grows in the volcanic soils of southern Mexico. It has long been used in the manufacture of Tequila, as well as an ingredient in many Mexican dishes for thousands of years.

After being heated to convert the carbohydrates to sugars, the syrup is sold as a healthy alternative to sugar.

No Mexican feast is truly complete without the country's signature cocktail. It is so simple and so fresh that, once you get the right ingredients, I guarantee it will become a staple of your summer evenings. The lemon and lime juices must be freshly squeezed — no pre-made mixes here, please.

margarita tradicional
Benito's Hat margarita

lime wedge
rock salt, in a saucer
35 ml/1 generous oz.
   Tequila Blanco
25 ml/1 oz. Triple Sec
2 teaspoons agave syrup

25 ml/1 oz. fresh
   lemon/lime juice
   (half and half)
ice

cocktail shaker
cocktail glass

MAKES 1

Prepare the cocktail glass by rubbing the lime wedge around the rim and then pressing the glass upside down in the saucer of salt.

Put the Tequila, Triple Sec, agave syrup and citrus juice in the cocktail shaker with a generous scoop of ice. Seal and shake hard for 3 seconds.

Strain into the prepared cocktail glass over fresh ice and garnish with the lime wedge.

margarita de sandia
watermelon margarita

There are endless varieties of flavoured margaritas that you can make, but nothing embodies the summer quite like fresh watermelons. A little bit of fresh lime juice to cut the sweetness and you are all set. Don't forget to keep count though, as they have a habit going down a little too easily!

6 x 3-cm/1-in. chunks
   of watermelon, plus
   a wedge, to garnish
25 ml/1 oz. Tequila
   Blanco
15 ml/½ oz. fresh
   lemon/lime juice
   (half and half)
15 ml/½ oz. grenadine
ice

cocktail shaker
muddle stick (optional)
cocktail glass

MAKES 1

Put the peeled, seeded chunks of watermelon in the cocktail shaker and crush with a muddle stick or the end of a rolling pin.

Add the Tequila, citrus juice, grenadine and a generous scoop of ice. Seal and shake hard for 3 seconds.

Strain into a cocktail glass and gently push the watermelon wedge onto the rim of the glass.

*

TEQUILA is made from the agave plant and originates from the town of the same name near the west coast of Mexico. If you're going to make a real Benito's Hat margarita, the Tequila must be 100% blue agave – that doesn't need to be expensive, but it mustn't be very cheap!

margarita de cilantro
coriander/cilantro margarita

It may sound weird to use coriander/cilantro for a cocktail but hold your disbelief until you have tried this — after all, would you have thought to put mint and rum together for a Mojito?! This cocktail was the result of a few very fun hours experimenting with Ben when we wanted to come up with a special, seasonal cocktail for the restaurant.

1 small handful of coriander/cilantro leaves
35 ml/1 generous oz. Tequila Blanco
25 ml/1 oz. Triple Sec
1 teaspoon agave syrup

35 ml/1 generous oz. fresh lemon juice
ice

cocktail shaker
muddle stick (optional)
cocktail glass

MAKES 1

Crush the coriander/cilantro in the cocktail shaker with a muddle stick or the end of a rolling pin.

Add the Tequila, Triple Sec, agave syrup, lemon juice and a generous scoop of ice. Seal and shake hard for 15 seconds.

Strain into the cocktail glass over fresh ice.

margarita de granada
pomegranate margarita

Pomegranates are a beautiful fruit with a unique flavour. They are rich in vitamin C and potassium as well as being full of antioxidants. That means you can have a cocktail and do yourself some good at the same time!

½ pomegranate
25 ml/1 oz. Tequila Blanco
15 ml/½ oz. fresh lemon/lime juice (half and half)
15 ml/½ oz. Triple Sec

cocktail shaker
cocktail glass

MAKES 1

Hold the pomegranate half over a blender and tap the skin with a large spoon to encourage the seeds to drop out. Scrape out any remaining seeds. Add a spoonful of water and whizz for 20–30 seconds until juiced.

Put all the ingredients in the cocktail shaker with a generous scoop of ice, seal and shake hard for 10 seconds. Strain into the cocktail glass.

margarita de fresa
frozen strawberry margarita

35 ml/1 generous oz. Reposado
    Tequila
35 ml/1 generous oz. Triple Sec
15 ml/½ oz. agave syrup
100 g/⅔ cup strawberries, hulled
15 ml/½ oz. grenadine
a small scoop of ice cubes

MAKES 1

Keeping back 1 strawberry for
garnish, put all the ingredients in
a blender and whizz until smooth.
Pour into a glass. Cut a groove in the
strawberry and gently push it onto
the rim of the glass.

margarita de mango
frozen mango margarita

1 small mango
35 ml/1 generous oz. Reposado
    Tequila
25 ml/1 oz. Triple Sec
2 teaspoons fresh lime juice
2 teaspoons agave syrup
a small scoop of ice cubes

MAKES 1

Cut 2 thin wedges from the mango, to
garnish. Peel and pit the remaining
mango and finely chop the flesh. Put
all the ingredients in a blender and
whizz until smooth. Pour into a glass
and stand the mango wedges inside.

suppliers & stockists

UK

Condimentos La Mixteca
Fernando Fuentes Cruz (Felipe's brother) and Fortunata Cruz Lima (Felipe's mother) produce fantastic dried avocado leaves and salt, for cooking and for margaritas, using traditional methods. Available to supply wholesale anywhere in the world.

Visit their page at:
www.facebook.com/CondimentosLaMixteca

Condimentos
La Mixteca

All the Condimentos La Mixteca are available direct from www.mexgrocer.co.uk

www.mexgrocer.co.uk
This website stocks a large range of authentic, high-quality Mexican food products in the UK and Europe, including fresh and dried chillies, corn tortillas, hibiscus flowers, masa harina, epazote, corn husks for tamales and cooking sauces.

www.coolchile.co.uk
Cool Chile Company are another good purveyor of high-quality Mexican spices, chillies and tomatillos. They also make their own corn tortillas.

www.organicexotic.com
Organic & Exotic has a wide variety of hard-to-find, ethically sourced, Mexican ingredients including dried spices and pure fruit pulps in larger quantities and can provide you with information of local, smaller quantity stockists.

www.casamexico.co.uk
Suppliers of molcajetes and authentic tortilla presses as well as Mexican groceries.

US

www.mexgrocer.com
A good online source for hard-to-find Mexican herbs like epazote, Mexican oregano and Guajillo chillies as well as everyday staples for your Mexican kitchen.

www.avocadodiva.com
Online source of dried avocado leaves (hojas de aguacate).

www.chefscatalog.com
Search here for molcajetes and tortilla presses.

www.purcellmountainfarms.com and **www.bobsredmill.com.**
Look up either of these suppliers for artisan, stone-ground masa harina.

www.ansommills.com
Adventurous tortilla makers can order heirloom yellow hominy corn and culinary lime from Ansom Mills to grind and prepare their own masa harina.

www.melissasfarmfreshproduce.com
This is a good source for fresh tamarind pods, fresh epazote leaves and dozens of chilli varieties.

AUSTRALIA

www.fireworksfoods.com.au
Canned tomatillos, chillies, queso fresco, Mexican oregano, epazote, tortilla presses, molcajetes and much more.

index

acknowledgments

From the first time Felipe and I met in a hot kitchen in east London to now serving more than 1,000 customers every day, our journey has been wonderful, challenging and at times very stressful. Felipe's wife Siobhan and my wife Kay Lee have been a source of unwavering support throughout and we owe them a huge debt of gratitude. A big thanks must also go to our parents and family who have supported us from the very early stages, whether that be financially, emotionally, through stopping strangers in the street and telling them to come and visit Benito's Hat or, as is obvious from the pages of this book, inspirationally.

From the beginning, Ed David has been part of the Benito's Hat core team. A special thanks goes to him, John Fordham, Susan Harriman, Sam Coxe, Michelle Cox, Matthew Newman, Ed Mallet and Amparo Martinez who showed so much faith in our idea when it was just in black and white on a piece of paper.

We know that Benito's Hat would be nothing without its staff. They work hard and greet every customer with a smile no matter their real mood. Special mention must go to the chefs, both Benito's Hat and not, who have helped me develop and fine-tune the recipes in this book: Erick Medina, Carlos Zúñiga and Rolando Gómez.

We must also say a huge thank you to the many friends, old and new, who have provided us with advice and assistance as we struggled to cope with the ceaseless demands of starting a new restaurant. Special mentions go to Eric Desgranges who got me to Europe and began with me on this journey to achieving my dream; Dan Changer for his architectural and design contribution; Lucy Greenwood from MECCO who gave me my first job in the business and continues to be a great source of advice; Stephen Wall from Pho who, after nearly thwarting our first restaurant, has gone on to answer my many mundane questions; and Sally Bishop of Relish PR for her early advice and ideas.

Also thanks to Peter Cassidy for making our food look beautiful in this book, and to Céline, Megan and the rest of the team at Ryland Peters & Small who took a chance on us.

Finally, thank you to all our customers. Everything we do is made worthwhile when we see a customer coming back for a second, third or fourth visit. Please keep coming and we will keep working as hard as we can to bring you great Mexican food every day of the week.